Inscribing My Name

Inscribing My Name

Selected Poems
New, Used, and Repossessed

Herbert Woodward Martin

Foreword by W. D. Snodgrass

The Kent State University Press
Kent, Ohio

© 2007 by The Kent State University Press, Kent, Ohio 44242
Library of Congress Catalog Card Number 2006016313
ISBN-13: 978-0-87338-876-4
ISBN-10: 0-87338-876-3

Manufactured in the United States of America

10 09 08 07 06   5 4 3 2 1

Library of Congress Cataloging-in-Publication Data
Martin, Herbert Woodward.
Inscribing my name : selected poems : new, used, and repossessed /
Herbert Woodward Martin ; foreword by W. D. Snodgrass.
p. cm.
ISBN-13: 978-0-87338-876-4 (pbk. : alk. paper) ∞
ISBN-10: 0-87338-876-3 (pbk. : alk. paper) ∞
I. Title.
PS3563.A724I57   2006
811'.54—dc22   2006016313

British Library Cataloging-in-Publication data are available.

*This volume is dedicated to the sacred memory
of two poets, two colleagues, and one childhood friend without whose
affection I might never have survived.*

*Raymond R. Patterson (1929–2001)
Calvin C. Hernton (1934–2001)
Joseph S. McNamara (1941–2002)
John M. McCaffery (1939–2003)
William MacGee (1932–2004)*

*This volume is also inscribed with love for my daughters:
Sarah Elizabeth Altman Martin
Julia Johanna Martin
and my granddaughters:
Marina Sheree Worley
Christian Taylor Lovett
Athena Rose Croker*

*To my wife, my deepest affection
Elizabeth Susan*

Contents

Foreword

W. D. Snodgrass

The title of Herbert Woodward Martin's volume, *Inscribing My Name*, clearly foreshadows its central subject: the trials and difficulties of an Afro-American intellectual, the product of a broken home, in establishing an emotional life corresponding to his gifts as a teacher, poet, and reader (i.e., performer) of poetry.

The book opens with a cycle of twenty-one Antigone poems exploring the author's long-lasting desire and search for someone to fill such a role as Antigone took in the classical Greek tragedy—both in her care and guidance for her blinded father and in her determination to give her brother's body proper burial even at the cost of her own life. Thus each poem in this section is dedicated to someone whom Martin feels he "might have fallen in love with." Such constancy and dedication are, of course, so rare that it's not surprising his own deep needs for such a mate or partner lead him into what might seem to be inconstancies of his own and so into both grief and guilt. Later in the book, we will find a series of fourteen prayers which, in particular, ask forgiveness for this long search and the wrongs it has led him to.

The W. poems, though Martin labels them as "Pieces Toward an Autobiography," depict particularly the members of his parental family—his mother (whose family name was Woodward), his father, stepfather, and grandfather. Although his mother had suffered a severe stroke when he was very young, she survived for twenty-one years more and remained a major figure and influence on his life. Other poems here also deal with the father, David Nathaniel Martin, who separated from the mother when Martin was a teenager and died when Martin was in early adulthood. The second W. poem is dedicated to him and there are implied references in "The Deadwood Dick Poems," which tell about a legendary black cowboy whose real name had been Nathaniel Love. Immediately following this cycle is an excellent poem, "Coyote," also set in the cattle-herding West, but drawing heavily on what we've learned of Martin's father and so of the life, generally, of solitary black males.

Clearly, Martin himself has devoted much of his life to singing and to choir work. This, no doubt, has helped make him into a reader who can deliver a poem with great clarity and emotional power. Another consequence appears in a series of highly experimental and challenging poems, "Contrapuntal Pieces," each of which has at least two voices. These are interwoven, line by line; the first voice's lines start at the left margin, while the second's lines are always indented. In some cases the voices may hold different views; in others, one voice will deal with the details and specifics of a situation while the second may deal with its moral implications. Either voice alone would yield a rather simple and straightforward meaning; but by continually countering or reinforcing each other, they yield a much richer sense. In this more complex realization, one's mind is held and focused for longer on the scene or problem the poem projects. Occasionally, a reader may be uncertain whether to follow a line with the next in that same column or to move to the opposite column; we have an uncertainty not unlike what we face when drawn by our own differing motives and urges in facing the real world's dilemmas.

But I should not leave one with a sense that this collection is entirely composed of such cycles of related poems; there are, in fact, quite a few single poems only minimally related to others, though no less inventive and delightful for that—I have mentioned "Coyote" above. Still others may be completely individual in either subject matter, style, or tone. I would draw attention, particularly, to "Phone Message Found on a John Wall," "Ginkgo Trees," "The Serendipitous Cat," and, most especially, "Sassy Music."

Author's Note

When I looked back at my five previously published volumes, I discovered that I had begun several poetic sequences. Over the years they had increased in vision and perspective. So instead of ordering each of the volumes as they first appeared, I arranged all of the poetic sequences together, perhaps to show their growth and development. I have left the single poems in the order in which they first appeared. I have resisted the temptation to repair and revise these poems in order to make them seem as if they were written all as one piece. I have, essentially, left them as they were, when they were written, in order to give the poems a natural sense of growth. I can only hope to not have failed in this intent.

The chronological order of my first five books is as follows:

New York the Nine Million and Other Poems
The Shit-Storm Poems
The Persistence of the Flesh
The Forms of Silence
Galileo's Suns

Perhaps I should first explain how I came to choose the above titles. For the first book, it was simply a matter of raising the population of New York City to make it important in terms of population and culture.

My second book's title was influenced by three quotations. The first quotation came from Eldridge Cleaver's *Soul On Ice*. The second quotation came from Richard Wright's "The Ethics of Living Jim Crow." The third quotation comes from the African American Spiritual "Been in the Storm So Long."

The title of my third book uses a quotation from "The Outing" in *Going to Meet the Man* by James Baldwin.

The title for the fourth volume came from my studies in a graduate linguistic class where I learned that the Inuits have a word denoting fifteen forms of silence.

The title for my fifth volume came from my imagining that Galileo looked, maybe, once too often through that telescope and saw not one sun but many.

I was given a Siamese cat when I first lived in New York City. I gave the cat the name Antigone because the Greek character appears in *Oedipus Rex* as a devoted daughter to Oedipus, to family, and to God above all other callings. Perhaps I was thinking that cats were that devoted as well. Although I fought attachment to the cat, I did learn to care for it. When the cat was no longer with me I took on its characteristics, and so the Antigone poems were born.

In my youth I fell in love with many women thinking they might make marvelous wives or lovers. They became neither; many of these women were only brief acquaintances, but their charm, beauty, and personalities made me think they would make superb partners. So each of those women became the inspiration for the Antigone poem dedicated to her. Most of these women are somewhere in my secure past and, perhaps, are dead or do not know that a poem with their name exists. This is as it should be.

The Contrapuntal poems come from my New York City days when I sang oratorios and cantatas in choirs around the city. J. S. Bach is clearly the main influence for my attempting to write these poems. I came to believe that if a four-part chorus could sing together and be understood, why not two or more voices reading together? I also came to believe that the contrapuntal poem was a representation of eastern and western cultural ways of writing. In the western world we write from left to right; in the eastern world we write from right to left. Thus each of these poems may be read, independently, phrase for phrase down the left side and then down the right side. They may be read together in alternating sequence. Then they may be read backwards. After working this portion of the principle out, Fred Reading, a friend I met while studying at State University of New York at Buffalo, suggested that the contrapuntal poems worked every way but backwards. That freed me from a dead end. The range of possibilities became endless again. The contrapuntal poems were, for all intents and purposes, experimental. Once I reached "Contrapuntal No. 7" the gates were open again. One could read left right in alternating fashion down the page and then backwards, up the page. When I came to write "Contrapuntal No. 10," I wanted to write something technically memorable, and so I used a palindrome for the right side of the poem. Thus, one could read the right side of the poem word for word down the page and word for word backwards. It has caused no earthquakes.

I started writing the W. poems somewhere after 1965, when my mother had a stroke and Joseph Fennimore, the pianist and composer, sent me some money to help me out during those troubling months. That is how this sequence began. As I grew more and more confident I realized that there was a good deal of material in my family that could be mined and turned into poems. When my family left the south, I thought never to look back at that time in my life ever again. Luckily, something encouraged me to open the door to those experiences. I have never regretted opening that Southern door. In section VI of this poem the reference is to the French composer Olivier Messiaen and not to Jesus Christ or to the second coming.

In an attempt to find new subject matter and a voice near my head or community, I turned to the black cowboy, and as a result "The Deadwood Dick Poems" were born. The name James Thomas Crowe is used several times in this work. I am making a reference to Jim Crow and Uncle Tom. I have tried to dignify and give importance to the name by adding a final "e."

The following is a list of miscellaneous notes about poems that the reader may find helpful:

- In "Antigone III," *Butterfly* is a reference to Giacomo Puccini's *Madam Butterfly*.
- In "Antigone IV," Jose Ortega y Gasset was a twentieth-century writer and philosopher.
- In "The Deadwood Dick Poems," Philharmonic Hall is a part of the Lincoln Center for the Performing Arts. Gustav Mahler was the nineteenth-century Austrian composer of the song cycle *The Songs of the Wayfarer.*
- In "American Confessional," William Billings was an eighteenth-century American composer.
- In "Coyote," "Surrender" was the ex-slave's way of referring to the end of the Civil War. It not only suggests that the South lost the war but that they had to surrender as well. Henry Beckwith was a black cowboy.
- In "W. Poem," Charlie McCarthy was ventriloquist Edgar Bergen's dummy.

- In "W. Poem II (a)," Robert Duncan was a twentieth-century American poet.
- In "W. Poem III," Olivier Messiaen was a twentieth-century French composer.
- In "W. Poem VI," *A World of Light* is a nonfiction book by May Sarton, a twentieth-century American poet.
- In "Remembering Hyde Park," Hyde Park is in London, England.
- In "Memory Poem for the New Year," "My sweet jimmy" is a phallic symbol.
- In "The Spoils of the Day," Hopalong Cassidy, Roy Rodgers, and Gene Autry were singing actors in cowboy movies. Serials were popular movies usually shown in installments of twelve or thirteen chapters, with each of the previous chapters ending in a cliff-hanger. In the final installment good triumphs over evil.

"Out of the Dead Bones" is one of the many experimental poems I have tried to write on the spot with words written on a card that is given to me by the audience. The principle is to use all the words without censorship. No, I have not deleted a single word.

"Tight Rope Walking the Air" is written about the student habit of throwing pairs of shoes or sneakers over electrical wires. Originally I thought, at least in college communities, this act symbolized wastefulness. I have since learned that in other communities it denotes where the drug dealer lives.

In "You Shall Skip through This Museum: Life," Joan Miro was a twentieth-century French painter.

In "A Negro Soldier's Viet Nam Diary," the narrator uses the phrase "with all deliberate speed." The U.S. Supreme Court in 1954 also used this phrase when it declared that all southern schools should be desegregated "with all deliberate speed." This unwittingly became the escape clause for the south.

OEDIPUS TO ANTIGONE

Daughter! . . . Daughter!
I beg you, take my hands!
Teach them newly how to feel.
Encourage these sightless feet
To avoid the brick, escape the stone.
I plead you daughter, guide me to some blind exile
Where I might reason what structure emotion is when
Flesh is bare and scarred; the crown has toppled the head;
When façade falls, and bone begins to flake.

ANTIGONE I
for Shoko

Perhaps
This is the way
The world looks from the moon
If it has sight at all
To see me in my dreams
Loving your tiny sinews.

> Moon tighten sea,
> River run through grass.
> There is a pool of dust
> On the desert tonight.

Whatever light there is, comes from the false sight of the moon.
But consider as I do the past winter love, leaf to my finger.
There are winds that revolve around the stars.
There is a certain clarity to their sight,
Should they, too, chance to see. You must know that.
This year the losses are great: several Negroes; a number of whites;
One, Siamese, silverpoint, beautiful; all in a forest of grass.
Truly there was a love among us. So, the increment of vanity.
There is, however, a certain clarity to understanding possessions lost.
You, who lost a lover, that loss I know, remembering
There was a year when twice I lost a love
And have not touched that music again.

ANTIGONE II
Tavernpiece

There are too many colored lights . . . I depart between the colors
where too many faces are forcing themselves into a private reality . . .
There is a darkness that makes the shapes and forms of things
invisible . . . It is upon the gold of beer that the world spins . . .
I tremble when I think of all the things I want privately to whisper
to you . . . This world is too public . . . We spin out our lives
in the noise of our minds . . . Your mouth is the thin difficulty of
porcelain . . . It is a lonely business addressing truth . . .
There is so much talk running counter to what I am thinking . . .
This public world becomes the shout of my whisper . . .
Do you know what I want to say? It hangs in my throat like
the instrument that rings the bell . . . *It is important to cry.*

ANTIGONE III

Now when I remember our conversations, they seem futile—
There was nothing to be achieved by them.
You could not conceive how much I loved you when you spoke to my ear
Nor can you know what a silence exists in my heart now.
We are measured by the lines of our truth.
So much of what you talked of I have not distinguished lie or truth.
"Lie" is such an offensive word to you . . . but it does have life.
I am in and out of this strange music.
I am measured from measure to measure.
I watched how you, a prima donna, playing *Butterfly*
For other reasons, pulled all the stops . . .
On any proscenium stage the critics would have
Acclaimed you under the heading tour de force
But not knowing you, nor seeing your drama on the level of their bodies
They were not equipped to judge. Some theatre is too close.
There is a sufficiency about an acquaintance with pain.
I know the circumstances, your natural reasons for playing *Butterfly,*
And in what particular time the measures of your music should be heard.

ANTIGONE IV
for Ann Robbins

He has looked enough in service at her window, Ortega y Gasset.
She is never there to his eyes. There is the distinct possibility
That she never was; that if there is a motive to love they will
Never finger it among formal figures.
There is less ability to say: "Love, there are certain conditions
We cannot have . . ." You exhaust the heart with such a truth.

He sits and cleans one fingernail with another—
The rain begins to destroy the possibility of leaves—
The voice in his head moves music through water.
There is no regret at loving a simple music.
He searches the annoyance that burns his ear.
There are certain conditions we cannot have, Ortega y Gasset.
This particular love never knew its dying.

ANTIGONE V

I knew the first warmth beneath Shoko
Now the soft face lies adapted.
Woman, you have become with your hair
Clipped and teased into newer modes, Bizarre!
These fashions covet your old existence.
Have you not felt them covering your past like Helena
Rubinstein, who allows a natural glimpse at the faults
In the face, covers it in tans and browns so you will not
Be whitewashed into the scenery you move about?
Seeing you again, I converse with myself.
I accept the new relationship.
I go walking the street blocks until I am too tired.
I fall irretrievably upon the single arm of my bed.

ANTIGONE VI
(All day walking with a yellow rose)
for Rachel,
a girl in Central Park

I choose not to walk among ghosts
(The wind this summer moves softly over the voices of children)
or with the young girl in the purple gown,
with mascara eyes, distributing yellow roses
as if they were answers.
She is as blatant as the sun.
Velvet is the metaphor of her rose.
The stem has thorns, on which flesh will bleed
(even when the children's voices are gone.)
and murder its odor.

ANTIGONE VII
for Joanna

I write intoxicated because . . . you have too often
teased me into other worlds and times . . .
otherwise I might never voice
these moments that move my mind . . .
I dream in a bed . . . in a room
not bounded by walls . . . sleep is still possible . . .
It is the fuse that guides the fire . . .
So slowly I burn my candle down . . .
Walk quietly with me
through these nervous recollections . . .
I will tell you that sin
(as naked as we lay
in the late afternoon)
will find no blood to slip into
to be redeemed by . . .
We are not requited . . .
shy . . . shamed . . . inhibited . . .
speaking only as we can
through outward movement . . .
We must start to peel the paint off
the walls to find what is underneath.

ANTIGONE VIII
Tavernpiece
for Judi

Some feelings are impossible to touch . . .
They are like . . . in the mid-afternoon
once, while listening to Spanish songs,
when the yellow sun blazed through the blinds bringing with it
the form of black leaves,
I could hear the music, see the vision,
move my hands through the space,
shadow displacing shadow . . . some feelings are impossible . . .
You, woman, who are so lovely in your haste,
what are you like when you are still,
when you do not have to move so swiftly from table to table?
Here in your world where people order bottles of dreams,
how do you keep all their possibilities in mind?
They are like the reflections that streamed through my window
once, in the mid-afternoon . . . What Italian master cut your face in flesh?
How well you have kept his art!
How do you walk in the 3 A.M. air? Is it fresh to you?
Do you have other arms to walk you in warmth?
Beer always spins my mind, weaves it, catches it
in a multitude of possibilities . . . like sunlight and form of leaves . . .
It is a vision the hand cannot hold.

ANTIGONE IX
for Helen

I have seen love pass my lips,
Move out of my hands
Like air you cannot hold,
Away from the circle of my eyes.

If you ever consider what I have become
You may perceive me in your fear
Free and tender, know
I can never touch the reality of you,
Only embrace you close in the imagination.
But the imagination cannot hold
Unless fortified by stone.

I would grasp the stone
If there is any.

ANTIGONE X

Antigone, begins to curious
the fragments and the encounters
the women who
fell attractive to the eye
anonymous as felt air
alert as lovers,
we travel gravely with our single secret Cat.
There are not enough coffins for the quiet
registered somewhere in a third of my brain,
between vision and memory, city and air.

ANTIGONE XI
for Elizabeth

I have come close to moments of possibilities, where
What I have wanted to say was more than the curve of lips.
Thus, while I visit in this room warm to my senses,
I desire you to dream by.
That man who would know the truth of what he perceives must gamble.
There are stronger men in flesh than I am Antigone.
The travel toward love is a long way.
Perhaps, discovery is too much concerned with the heart.
I should not expect too much of silence,
Of what the eyes speak,
But when the mouth does not move
One must touch and know the force of breath.

ANTIGONE XII

Man, the body is a map of ruined sense
That risks its five particular visions to feel.
Go break a stone in half, see if any water is there,
Find a heart that beats, and question it about love.
It will give you no definite facts,
It realizes: The wind can usher grief through tragedy,
That fire can rupture the mind,
A song can distill the flesh.
Man, you can charter countries,
Discover the road to the spirit is through the flesh
But only the five distinct senses can lead you there.
If you pull a bird apart
You will destroy its song.

ANTIGONE XIII
for Atalissa Gilfoyle

Love drives us where the soul aches most.
Antigone I know!
I have gone single-handedly to that periphery:
Where I have tried to exorcize darkness deep
Like the descent of a woman's thighs;
Stood the fire that burns without source
While it ravages every hair upon my skin that
No water can quench, nor rain redeem.
Love spares neither flesh nor bone
We leave all brief encounters hard.

ANTIGONE XIV

In Rembrandt's town a young man and his woman
Joy in each other under the veneer of two vital days,
Then separate: she to Paris, he to Amsterdam.

The rain falls inside him all night long.
Longing is the clear descent of water-drops.

At some point between sleep and morning
The rain stopped; the body rested.
The morning air fresh and chill
Awakens him to another day.

A butterfly moves expectantly in the sun.

ANTIGONE XV

I have knelt by the knees of many women.
It is not as if I have not made proposals
Out of the blood's necessity, but
Their palms always turn me away.
How am I to move beyond expectation?
Shall I worship until I become saint and stone?
Saint and stone like brother and sister are from the same flesh.
They have spirit but no pulse.
So easily and lustfully I fall in love with the flesh.
It is the hand which shuts the door of passion against me.
O Antigone; I would not be saint, I would not be stone.
Where would you have me flesh my prayers?

ANTIGONE XVI
for Barbara

I do not trust the voice of men.
The space between
The spoken word and hearing is defective.
You can brush past the air
But never touch the image
Imprisoned in silver.
The heart aches most when
We cannot give it away.
I freely bequeath body, breath, and pulse to your bed.
O Antigone,
We are so cautious moving toward death.
These are the nights I desperately spend.
You know the love is there,
You know it is honest.
You will not take it to your bed.
Love singularly makes us suffer the most.
Corrupts like death,
And breaks, breaks the tenuous sounds
We would be sure of.

ANTIGONE XVII
for Betty

The girl who plays with her navel is black.
Her skin is polished, is smooth as breast.
Shall I kiss her there and tell her that
She tells me things she is unaware of?
I hear through my eyes.
I speak with my hands.
She walks through her eyes out the window.
The day is dreary. It surrounds us.
The sun is out somewhere above the clouds.
We cannot see that far into the day.
Sitting here across from each other,
There are too many years between us.

ANTIGONE XVIII
(Tavernpiece)

Antigone beer
courses through me like a river
freshly through mountains or under-
ground streams that break gently through the earth.
The smoke in taverns aches my eyes.
I watch a young man peruse his girl with his fingers.
I think I shall go out into the wind and accept
the challenge of love, otherwise I shall write
a million fantasies about leaves on water.
Sit close to me woman;
be next to me like a stab of pain in the heart.
Rip my flesh; love is buried in my bones.
It aches to rise and become my skin,
follicle and hair frightened.
Oh, the rush of love is pain.

ANTIGONE XIX
for Marie

Antigone
There are those times when expectations turn
The sweet taste to salt, when nothing
Of the advanced news occurs,
The valued moment never appears.
I cannot tell you what pain accrues in my flesh.
It grows in interest like the roots of hair in my skin.
It utters forth like a rejection from the stomach.
It hardens like a callous underfoot,
And speaks to me of pain
When I step in treacherous places.

ANTIGONE XX

Water is my mirror
Water is my death
Air my heavy breath.
I cannot see my heart
I cannot hear my pulse
I cannot taste my salt
Nor smell my flesh
Nor feel my dust.
A noise like regret blinds
My fragile eyes like light
Stabbed through crystal
As it moves from love to love.

ANTIGONE XXI

Nothing is written in the earth, yet I perceive its history.
I am no farmer; I turn the land with my hands.
I set my passions out in strict regimen,
Hope what seeds I plant will take the sun, will root
And hold for themselves and the land their place
Or in time neighbor some luscious fruit.
There are no elements like fire, none like water;
The earth is a place where men may harvest the air.

CONTRAPUNTAL PIECE NO. 1
A Fable of Two Thoughts
for Sally

Around the corner from where I am,
        If I could tell you what love is I would
A young man stands in his waiting.
        Once I thought it fleeting past my door
Down a summer's street a girl, becoming woman, comes closer.
        Possessed the glimpse in the eyes' crevice.
They will seize each other's existence.
        I do not know what love is
"Lady," he will say, "the smell of your black hair
        Suspect I never will,
The touch of your lips against my collar-bone,
        Since my too brief gaze at the soul has
Attract, the strength of me."
        Vanished between the lines of sunrise and twilight
If lovers can love and feel no shame
        Ambivalence is the emotion between these lines
They can part and feel no duty.
        Where sunrise and twilight guard
        The soul-secret in its primeval.

CONTRAPUNTAL PIECE NO. 2
A Smile, a Hand, a Heart: Love Begins This Way

You are on the right.   I am on the left.

Opposition.   Counterpoint.

THIS HAS NOTHING TO DO WITH MORALS.

Are you saying?   Recommending.

Is it . . . ?   Sorrow?

Gravel against grain,   We counter

Each other's emotion.   Content yourself

THERE IS NO MODERATE GROUND.

We stand at too far a distance

The distance is too far for hands

BEST, THE HEART SPANS SPACE.

Does it?   Does it.

I contemplate you on hectic ground

Yet, if the heart gestures, the element is in the sound

No, in the graph that moves up, moves up, moves down

Speak individual, not for other men

Where truth resides   Emotion is a word

The ear positive to hear   The eye is sure to see

The tongue definite to speak

TRUTH, THEN, IS A STATE OF MIND.

CONTRAPUNTAL PIECE NO. 3
Man   Woman

I. a round

I thought as we were walking opposite ways

     I thought as we were walking opposite ways

One of us might have turned, called to the other

     One of us might have turned, called to the other

A sentence of reconsideration, yet, less by less

     A sentence of reconsideration, yet, less by less

The obvious turn over distance withers irrevocably.

     The obvious turn over distance withers irrevocably.

II. contrapuntal

Now are we of a particular hope, prisoners.

     Swift, fall leaves the stone-walk.

We claw up essential ladders.

     We walk down an autumn.

Despite what seems, and what is not legitimate

     Nuance is an interminable path.

Let us say in recollection,

     As we become the variant,

Each rung is a step toward

     A strife of light,

The expanse of all our distances,

     Falls cataract on our eyes

And our hopes are all that is left of a continuum.

CONTRAPUNTAL PIECES FOR CENTRAL PARK WEST NO. 4
for Tom Howard

I

Pausing in the bend of a corner
      If the fiction must be told
To windowshop himself come and gone
      This is the way it ought to read
There was a man walking Negro
      He is sitting on wood and stone
Down where he trembled
      Seeking to intrigue you with the level of his eyes
Under the edge of his mind
      Deep beyond the cornea
Gazing upon prospect,
      Where emotion paces this sidewalk
Realizing, alone, the night is long
      Discovering a remote frailty
Being driven to companion it by twelve
      He admits only to the darkness of his palm
Dimensions with that bruised secret.
      Beneath an extinguished street lamp
He cripples his feet to the form of pavement,
      Affords himself a dream of warmth and brandy
Knowing end is always caught in distances
      To calm the effect of waiting
And beginnings lie vaguely on the tip of the tongue.

II

I suffer that body which is intimately yours
      In particular moments of our genesis
Having felt you where my depth lies
      He bears your pain as you his love
Deep within our separate discoveries
      So much of you exists in whispers
That I confess pulse-breath
      Between the dream and the act.

CONTRAPUNTAL NO. 5
In the Very Savage Fall
for Joseph Fennimore
with the most precious thing I know

In the very august of the mind
        When savage fall the time of rain
The plumb that seeks the depth
        In glass puddle, eyes see a room
Finds the circle hollow beneath
        The exquisite extreme of manners
The strenuous rising of the moon.
        While later wind sorrows the water on.
We rest shoulders in the grass
        The base hammer, the pain
Willow a kiss upon the throat
        Inhales the breath, releases the cry
Stir the common realm that
        Staves the torture in the blood
Turns the wheel, the pulse, rhythm
        Parts the eyelids, wracked focus
Of the womb, the vast crawl,
        Begins through the distorted pupil.
The journey through the motherbone.

LINES TOWARD A FORMAL FEELING

(Contrapuntal No. 5 ½)

for Sheila Hartman Hughes

I

That afternoon we saw each other, indulged in trivialities
(Talk, laughter, smiles, gestures, coffee, doughnuts)—
Then it was time for her to go.
I watched her board the bus,
Heard, "I shall be home Saturday."
I turned into the station,
Passed the table where momentarily we sat,
Reconsidered our simplicities . . . thinking Saturday
Forced my thoughts to move at the level of my feet.
I would wait.

II

Today it will rain, snow, or storm some element
        In the violence of my room, I have had enough of silent winters
At the sharp distance of consideration
        I shook in abstract winds
Where someone practices his theory of the stars
        But the condition is as it was before genesis
There are no voices, the mind is disenchanted.

III

The vessels that hold my blood scream you song
Dream of skin, green, rape of distract
Strangled in its pitch, drowned in the factor of blood.
I beg more than dream, more than imaginings
Creating you here in this room, there in the bed
Soft to my flesh, silent, except for breathing.
We taste:
        the full move through exploration;
        vast afternoons in the balance of love
        accosting our singular sense of evening;
        sleep, in the heavy arms of summer silences.

CONTRAPUNTAL NO. 6

for Janet Willer,
who asked for a poem

Standing here in what seems like a difficult moment
        We are destroyed by too rough a touch
All in the mind runs the pleasure of love
        Never sensing the condition of our coming
Orpheus sang in his death upon frigid water
        Such truth can puncture the heart
It is a difficult form of harmony
        Listening only to the head sing
Where intellect struggles to assess its estate
        And song has lost the motive of blood
In that special time called now
        We should have remained filed in exile
In the condition of Orpheus's singing
        Love, we never heard the fire in his voice.

CONTRAPUNTAL NO. 7
for Fred Reading

And do you wonder why
                 in those last two months
we came to touch so close
                 I found an allowance of courage
fearing neither kiss nor embrace
                 to drive my image straight
hungering between two worlds?

CONTRAPUNTAL PIECE NO. 8
for the young women at Marywood Academy

After the rooms where you have held your breath
      It may not be you nor your sound mad in the mind
In strange places where no light shines
      That frays the flesh, only start and finish
It is enough to know the moment was infinitely possible
      A man must sometime be his own antagonist

CONTRAPUNTAL PIECE NO. 9
for Leo

Somewhere I have promised never to make music again
                  In my winter love there is so much desperation
Because the flesh does not always burn by fire
                  I hate to acknowledge the hungers of my body
The first sense of pain is what paralyzes
                  I am a man whose soul walks the dreadful air
We can count all objective things
                  I have dreamed my own soul's prison
There is no beginning except with truth
                  I am a thief born remarkably into hell
Gradually, an animal becomes the body it digests
                  The heart will stop when it is devoured

CONTRAPUNTAL PIECE NO. 10

In Memoriam
Paul Laurence Dunbar (1872–1906)

Truth like the sun will burn if you stand too close
    Five summers my flesh I memorized Brahms
Between two points lie the crooked paths
    Girls waiting long realized
Sorrow I love beyond my natural means
    Walking eternal is music
All men move specific in time
    As man must surely die
Love is like the smell of cut grass
    Wind pause silence comes suddenly
The head knows nothing lasts
    Drop by drop, dripping water measure, time

CONTRAPUNTAL PIECE NO. 11

The rain perforates the air and ground,
> In Milan the hours go quickly now.
I want wine and food and then love,
> What care shall I take for Wednesday?
For the days after will insure themselves.
> I have a few good memories in my heart.

CONTRAPUNTAL PIECE NO. 12

for Lorraine Murphy

Let the body absorb the shocks
>> In the palm, the grace of night lingers, still

Omit nothing the eye perceives
>> Stand sideways, couch no fear in the eye

Omit nothing the hand longs for
>> Let the body absorb the shocks

The heart is an emotional fact
>> The moon will bear you utterly.

CONTRAPUNTAL PIECE NO. 13
for David M. Pahnos

Beneath certain darkness where no light fell
        This night was all the shadow of the moon
I know what terrors I have wrestled with
        When the door of morning reason opens
I find myself destitute in the blindness of many wars
        So quickly does the shadow retreat that
Among the devastation of many bodies
        I am not likely to learn where the night went
I am not likely to discover where the rain goes.

CONTRAPUNTAL PIECE NO. 14

Smile do not hesitate, let us comfortably question
> In a dream where we are principle actors

What it is that supports the waters of the world
> Our naked testimony is a chalice for time

What is the cup that contains the miracle of breath
> Let us learn what intelligence this minute offers

We are requited; we seek the same answers
> The earth is the altar whereon we may rest

CONTRAPUNTAL PIECE NO. 15
At This Point in Time
  for my students, Fall 1977

My dears, it's nothing to me
                Hey, benefactor old man of the people
I make use of what I see
                In the absence of a formal definition
To establish a common meaning
                The art of declamation
The great man's imperturbable assurance
                Which the author knows, like the Shadow,
The military has expressed interest in
                The working competence of men
The secret ability to cloud men's minds
                They will suffer no sense of defeat
They pin their faith to material interests
                There is no doubt that sooner or later
That's so universal as to lose significance
                (In the maintenance of reducing downtime)
More perhaps by inference than by definition
                That procedure must give insight by design

CONTRAPUNTAL PIECE WITHOUT NUMBER

I do not know how to tell you this
My daughter prefers donuts to asparagus
    Blunt, direct, straightforward without metaphor
With heavy German cream, thick Hungarian jams
    Bread that is warm in Southern hospitality
Covered with layers of delicate Swedish pastries
    That sings of love and butter on the tongue
That walks the long route down the esophagus
    That sustains melody and bounces on the diaphragm
Finally gliding into the engine of the stomach
    That replenishes the body's system audaciously

SECOND UNTITLED CONTRAPUNTAL

Many loves ago last Spring
     The old house disappeared
Many loves ago last Summer
     Bulldozers bit into the foundation
Many regrets last Fall
     The cellar roots were scuttled
Many pains ago last Winter
     The residual hole was covered
Many comings ago this Spring
     A fruit began to flower
Many harvests before this Summer
     The trees budded new houses
Many endings ago this coming Fall
     The earth continued to play the blues.

ANCIENT ELEMENTS
(Third Contrapuntal without Number)

In the mercy of the sun
      something is always attempting to bloom something
In the grip of suspicious rain
      something is always sprouting in the earth something
In the magnetic dust of storms
      something is always hazily settling something
In the sweet ease of wind
      something is always moving toward something

SO GREATLY WROUGHT
(Fourth Contrapuntal without Number)

The hours and days
                 In the lives of men and women
Transpire as lessons to change
                 The entire current of energy
The wash of circumstance
                 Of electrical sins
That towels wonder
                 Engenders in them a power
That dry simple beads of thought
                 To enlighten whole universes
By inserting crystal plastic
                 Intravenously back and forth
Into the pores of their human skin.

NEW YORK THE NINE MILLION

for Irene Neuman

I

Midnight.
Sleep until twelve.
Buy your paper now.
Sex is not to be had
For free or purchase.
Go home like a defeat from war
Masturbate,
It is the only sedative left:—
Take it . . .

II

One o'clock.
On West 8th and Sixth, watch
The man pace, where
The curb wears into the gutter.
A woman will come, if he can
Keep the matches dry long enough:—
She comes a long way for "A match, buddy?"
O nail yourself to your sheets
O nail yourself face down
Kiss into whatever breasts are there
It is the only sedative left:—
Take it . . .

III

Two o'clock.
I start home.
For my wife I will be the sedative;
Second her motion to love, and
Sleep to revival time.

It is a long way through my eyes,
From West 8th to West 125th.
Every voice in the subway
Has its own train.

Watch the man who looks in the mirror.
Watch him play the witch's trick.
Mirror, mirror, what am I?
Comb your hair,
Lick your lips,
It is the only sedative left:—
Take it . . .

IV

Morning.
To begin is holy.
Sunday is the idea of a sun splintered on pilgrims.
In Central Park the mind is not forced to cast a shadow.
Its religion is to relax.
That is its only sedative.

V

Noon, and after.
About goodness, a final point must always be made.
With a week's blessing in heart
I walk up through my eyes from 65th to 125th
See the buggied babies fighting the flies, while
Their nannies, white nannies
Push me up, push me down,
Pray all the gray-haired people
               who peek in
Lose their frown.

VI

A man came from behind and spoke to me.
"For my ache, could you spare a nicotine?"
"Sorry, I don't smoke."
There is no pity in refusing.
I touched his hand; left a quarter there,
Enough to make his knee go supple as prayer,
It may have been his only sedative:—
I left him in the nineties, thinking
A confusion of thoughts:
   rain:—
   sundown:—
   of pity and pain:—
That with Sunday's end the week has begun again.

THE DEADWOOD DICK POEMS
for Judith Brown Yales

I
Between the spaces,
Deadwood Dick
I vision you, man
Image within the pupils
Struggling somewhere in mid-life against the stampede
Odds of Texas, Arizona, Nebraska,
Horses and other men.
You, with your love of the free and wind,
The best eye on the plain
I have found it necessary to walk through your blood,
Question tender and desert nerves that
You might have preferred to deal with privately.

II
Early your father died.
He made you man at twelve
Through death, through the discipline
Of breaking colts for 10¢ a piece.
It was another horse
With which you earned your reputation and fee.
Too bad you lost your 25¢ by
Collecting it beforehand.
That animal-will which
First introduced you to stampede,
The rough paths and pasture;
That throttled you almost to the ground,
Taught your arteries tenacity.

III
You, Deadwood, master of rope and gun,
When the wind interrupts your sleep
The ground, I know, in that instance is harder.
I sense, what your nights must have been,
Where even the sagebrush approaching by wind
Is ultimately feminine company.

Although, that wind continues to move
Between you and your dreams
In the heat of its burning.

Deadwood what loneliness must have been like in those days!
One learns, in time, to sleep quite well alone.
I have experienced dust storms of the heart
Where you dig in and cover your face
Until the disaster is over or
You ride like hell through a hailstorm
Hoping the ice will not strike against your temples.
A man can shoot everything but nature.
When you were thirty,
Were you swift, learned, and happy,
As young men are supposed to be?
How many men did you know, who
Were afforded death by the natural stampede of your life?
Was the open as free as history records?

A man could shoot everything but nature
And death which itself is a bullet,
And loneliness, that knife of grass
Which cuts the flesh silently,
Although, the pain is apparent hours afterwards,
A man will resist everything if you tell him his heart is no good.

IV
Nat Love, in your black leather from foot to white Stetson,
You, man, were rough.
No woman's hand could have held you.
No circumstantial embrace could have kept you for more than a night.
What I want to ask is how . . . no, why?
After so many years of riding
You never recorded a single soft encounter?
Were there no quiet, accidental moments in barns?
Or everlasting evenings in the plains of flesh
Where, one lying next to another on the ground
Can hear the sound of everything approaching;
Feel the heat from gathered brush expire,

See the moon disappear,
Hear the wind stop.
Or fall deeper into sleep like night into silence?

There are certain concerns a man must be discreet about.

V

Deadwood, these are thoughts I put to you, ultimately,
Because I wish I could ride a black horse into history,
And desire to know if what you won by rope,
Horse, and gun was respect, rather than tussle?

There are individuals knocking at the gate of my brain
Who want to enter, separately.
Occasionally, I have escaped those social encounters
I have seen enough crimes against the body
I should like to ride out
Into the gallery of the world.
Men now-a-days will do one of three things:
Stare at you,
Shoot you to death,
Or brave up and reveal the pulse of their breath.
I am forced to entertain no one.
Relatively, in my private house, I continue to think all is safe.
Yet, a man must confide in something, or retreat.

VI

I have been listening to *The Songs of the Wayfarer*
Mahler knew, at least, what it was to wander.
Had he known you personally or otherwise
You might have inspired him
To write you a song cycle.
No doubt someone, preferably myself,
Would be singing your songs now.
I see it this way:
      TONIGHT
      In Philharmonic Hall
      James Thomas Crowe
      Will devote his American Debut to

The World Premier of Gustav Mahler's
DEADWOOD DICK LIEDER
I am thinking the critics would have said nothing less than:
"Moving"
"A monumental performance"
"A major song cycle"
"A major singer"
History, tells me your friends revered you like this, and
As I think Mahler might have.

History, should say the best it can about a man.

VII
In Tennessee you hunted rabbits.
In Texas, you learned men shoot men.
Deadwood Dick
Yours is a metaphor to exhaust.
The earth is not mother enough.
This earth this mother
She
Carnivorous devours us whole when we die.
We grow wise for that.
In Tennessee you hunted rabbits.
In Texas men learned you to shoot men.

VIII
Where are the dark wolves of your knowledge?
I question, you, Deadwood.
You may answer with subtle implications.
I know we have moved sufficiently from understanding.
So that to touch is less likely to mean love,
And to speak means certain death.
How do you feel in the open
With the moon's coyote gaze upon you?
Or when you wake and find a rattlesnake curled between your heart and
Stomach sleeping?
Where did you bury the knowledge of your dark enemies?

IX

Nothing seems dead about the photograph frozen in your lifetime,
You standing tough, foot on your saddle,
Your long black hair on your shoulders,
Shotgun in your left hand, and your cuffs rolled for work.
Do not let me invade your personal dreams:
They are the things which save us from bullets,
Snakes, men, and other dangers.
Young man, sometimes the stallion of your time will not give you a ride.
You must take a lariat, and tie him.
It gets neither of you anything.
You have no ride;
He cannot move,
And you must refuse to bear him upon your shoulders.
Sometimes, it is wise to say, a stallion is difficult to break.

You can look into the hands of a man ninety
And see the places he has traveled.

X

You Deadwood who
Woke one morning with Indians in your eyes,
Who suddenly turning from nightmare to tears
Bled real blood.
Exiting from that dream do you realize the cause may have been
That there was no woman to share the dawn with?
There is some excitement to be derived from riding a horse
But, a horse is never companion enough,
Not, at least, for a man named Nat Love.

Sunday night.
Deadwood,
The roads are deserted.
We discuss ourselves.

XI

James Thomas Crowe, dude, singer, actor, et al.,
went riding West
in search of history.

Carefully, Nat Love was overheard to say:
"Man, imagine
you come beating your ass out here
on a horse's back
talkin' 'bout questin'
for some kinda history or 'nother,
well,
I don't rightly know much about where it is
but it's out here
somewhere,
I guess
in the blood of the people
in the water of the land
between the length of life
inhale and exhale
which reminds me
speaking of life
'cause I ain't much on death
though don't get me wrong
I done seen a lot of men die
a heap more put away
life is something else!
I got an opinion there, now.
Man,
I tell you it's like
a bitch without a satisfying hound,
an occasional butterfly
that lights here and there
teases you but never lets you touch.
It is a rattlesnake with dust in its mouth.
That's what the rattler teaches.
If you do not busy the mind
the flesh will break down,
the spirit will run free of the body
like blood through an open wound.
If you would keep the soul, the flesh must suffer."

XII
Indians come in silence; buffaloes come with noise
Like maddened cowhands paid off and drunk,
Their sound comes first,
Then they appear and nothing can turn them around.

AMERICAN CONFESSIONAL

A song along the nerve

E. L. DOCTOROW

for Scott Rose

I think that   I want   to be direct   to be   as simple   as possible.
To take   the natural pattern   through unencumbered routes   over the
Rasp rugged tongue   through the cage of teeth   through the underbrush
Of syntax   to speak invisible words   and make sound tangible to the eye.
Out of the door   the sensuous mouth   the exit which   sometimes anger
And death   and sleep   can shut like a gage   devouring secrets
Even time is slow to reveal   from which   all common impulses proceed.

At night   the air is like a skin   that wraps itself   like a sudden
Lover in your arms   who lies like an exclamation in your bed where nothing
Of stress interrupts the linear passion   where the comma pulls back your breath
And the blind period renews the vision   where time seems neither predecessor
Nor successor   where light that exposes such secrets   astonishes the dawn.

I have consorted   in the secret closets of women   in the dark of their mouths
Drunk with demons   a wine dark and heavy   as the temperature of passion
To keep the tongue silent   concerning the marriage in the body the union of
Bone and cartilage   vein and artery   skin and flesh   brain and nerves
The ordinary function of liver and kidney   the forbidding knowledge of how
Intoxicating the simple touch can be   of its hereditary and lasting consequence.
It is evening   night touches my character   there is no repenting light
Sin is as indelible as pigment   a sudden common rattle in the rain
Leaves   like   death   a   silence   sorrows   in   me.

I know why great men waking   pray that their sleep was not madness
That their dreams   do not haunt them reoccurringly   like God and the Dark
Angel   contending   for our Father's first son. Sometimes after sleep   it is
A struggle   to command the body's senses   to ask the brain to consider:
The equilibrium   that helps foot and leg to function,   the human form which
Is   both   divine   and   amazing.

She   who came of age in sorrows   who carried me;   who felt me tunnel
To life   is apt and constant   in her reminders,   who learned early never
To borrow   is invalid,   old,   her hair the gray of years. She fears, I will

Shuttle her away   in some darkened place   this woman of dark sorrows
She is merciless and oppressive   like humidity and time.   It is not changes
That   affect us so   it is struggle   the inexorable   that will never   let go
For reasons   divine is   of the human form   amazing.

She of sorrows pursues me with many guilts sometimes to the gorge of death.
She of light   pursues me with pleasures   sometimes to the comfort of love.
Which draught shall I sip,   from whose cup?   I am forced to take from each
Her cup's full measure.   Herculean body   muscular and lean;   sinuous
loveliness   feminine dream; the mouth is split   sounds which spill forth
invite one to partake of extension and seam that touches man that tastes the
lips of a woman making the head, his being stands up between infinite
desire and stark   abstinence.   My male hunger   is governed by   the
darkest demon of sorcery. Influence   like inheritance in the blood   is the
excesses of man and woman divisible the best and worst passion and strife is
the   grounds   of   my   being.

Persevere to courage O mortal flesh   delineate to preserve intangible spirit
O sun wherein I dig my perfect place   O earth wherein I restore my mutable
Strength   O moon in whose shadows I disguise my miseries   My double eyes
Reveal no unique mysteries   my tongue has no sentiments to proffer
Only my nightmares those diversions of sleep that none may see O despair severe
And transitory flesh   O persevere courageous and invisible soul.

I seize this opportunity   before it passes   to set my heart (the human engine
That digests blood and air)   in the midst of that extraordinary activity
Which discriminates against infections and imperfections in the blood stream.
When the heart is in the common and dangerous air   it is subject to disasters
And corruption of the sun   like all things born of secrets and time.
Sometimes commending and commenting on the truth is as painful to the ear as night
Easy sounds   or a sudden sharp touch upon the spine   a pin shock of
Electricity   which stuns the body   in a stationary standing place.

When I see the morning sun which burns away all my human imperfections
And leaves my tangible mortal flesh   to contemplate the justifiable light
I become aware of that which lasts   that which remains mystery. When I see
The evening star whose calcium light vanishes like cancer devouring a nerve
I acknowledge   nothing will last   nothing stay.

The older the body grows   the more tallies it counts   the retiring   body
Retreating from the battle   recognizes its toll   tallies its inexorable
Wounds   contemplates the outrage   the consequence of war.

"When Jesus wept" (Billings) upon the rude wood, He came   destined to
Save my lost soul.   When He was placed in His earthly tomb   I leaned
Heavily into my sanity.   When He returned from His last mortal sleep it
Was for my spiritual offense.   When Jesus rose   in that enlightened hour
Never again   was   the   flesh   required   to   demonstrate   its   power.

All in my heart's treasure   my dreams   are kept separate   preserved
Distinct and apart   like darkness   held in the skull   like light
Gliding   through   the   eyes.
Once   love was the most, I could confess to   now I despair   with grief
As my mate   that ravaging maniac   who troubles the time stars dream   those
Special encounters   that never were. There is no returning   no discovery
Sought   no mirror of water   nor cool container   wherein truth may be seen.

My soul's possessor   nothing   when it is dying   can you save   can steel you
Against   a fire which cannot be felt   a flame which cannot be seen, whose
Form   rises   and   vanishes   in   the   invisible   air.
Sleep   prerequisite to temptation   arrest my temporary light   slide light
Into my prison   against the lock which holds captivity in place   let the
Day-birds continue to sing   let the woodpecker ground its song with tapping.

COYOTE
for John and Jean Pfiffer

I
Before Surrender, that war
when brother and neighbor
took aim at each other's life
to deliver each man's heart from body each man's soul from flesh
who set the issue of the land's dependence
on flesh which was bound and sold.

II
After Surrender which freed
in black script
on white paper
black men and their souls,
set them aimlessly on uncharted roads
allowed you Henry Beckwith
to wander into the west
alone.
The men who knew you
how you stepped and breathed
who watched your stealth and silence
called you
Coyote
animal whose game was hunt.

III
Coyote
stalks the stark
dark dense brush
where neither horse nor man
nor fleeing cattle
can see a yard ahead.
It is the scent
rope and guide
that leads the hunter.

IV
Coyote
digesting long stretches of air
breathing silences
learning the night's rhythm
the pulse and flight of the hunted
huddling over a small fire
whose light wards off fears
whose heat burns the cold away.

V
Coyote
alone
no partner to track with
to drink harsh chili-coffee with
or sleep in cattle runs
on earth, sticks, and horseblanket
covered by the cool moon.
Coyote
what animal keeps your watch
when the night grows weary?
The wisest course for a man
is to say nothing when hunting
or making love.

W. POEM
Pieces toward an Autobiography
  for Gordon Hibberd

I

Mother it was deep into mid-night when I heard you had fallen
ill with a stroke. I spent the late hours before morning
pacing prayer in the close dark of my heart.
We change in the circumstance of time as best we can.

When you lost your balance, the citizens you said,
found you amusing, stumbling toward death.
In the haste of Monday morning they remained thoroughly suspicious
about you who they thought had extended your weekend past their
    pleasure.
We look desperately upon the small articles of circumstance.

I look over the photographs hung in the corridors of your house,
touch a memory here and there to acquaint myself sufficiently
with your adjacent time, correlate those histories light should
touch upon, and allow what is contained in this house
to consider your possible passing.
I know certain winds braze the flesh.
I have seen the moonlight search a stone.
A grain of water will insist upon a seed.
Walking through these rooms disturbs the dust,
breaks the cobwebs, splinters the heart,
and hardens the marrow. Tears blind the vision.

I catch the wind and clouds in my eyes these days Mother.
That is the way truth is.
I catch the sun, also, in my eyes.
I cannot distinguish between the tears of the elements and the heart.
Things are sometimes that difficult when we pray.
If I were permitted Mother to tell you of my single madness
I would say I have spent hours of formal smiles, that
I possess a clown's image, that mastery of it lies
in fitting my face to the mold. It is a strange music
played in a different key from your rhapsody.

II

After I was conceived, before I was born
that portion which made me issue and heir
my father contributed, then died.
I am acquainted with the surface of dice.

III

My stepfather who
hyphenated his surname to mine
was all the father I knew.
I think, to bleed the figures of memory.
I could never talk of Sis. George, whom my stepfather slept with.
It is an old argument
which, perhaps, my childhood conceived incorrectly.

Mr. George did
give me a Charlie McCarthy doll
in that curious time
when boys can touch such things with impunity.
I never mastered the replica.
Somewhere, in our attic
it now lies covered in a box
under a history of dust,
bowed in with cobwebs.
It remains in its black coat,
checkered trousers,
burdened with that public smile.
Reluctance refuses
to touch such memories.

IV

My grandfather was a man of many talents,
so constantly my mother told me.
He hummed
the dominance of his history into a ceramic jug
which in later years
could not survive the intensity of our attic.
They say my grandmother moaned
the gradual of that history.

No tongue tells the taste of love.
No bloom speaks past pealing.
Mythically, he was a lover who touched the guitar.
When nothing else survives the memory,
there is no way back to Alabama to mourn.

V

Cousin, life is a constant source of madness
although I live beyond the fatal year for Christ.
I have not discovered a woman singular to my influence.
I have tasted a vision of alternatives.
I have had pleasure in savage suspicions.
I grasp
at the potential years of my genius;
believe in
the martyrdom upon the wood;
listen to my mythical grandfather's singing;
regard my hyphenated name;
observe the dice my father touched
and wait for
the last measures of the rhapsody to resolve,
cousin.

VI

Friend the honesties I
left unsaid at 36 West 95th!
We never stretched our speech to childhood cadences.
That music is unnecessary now.
It is difficult to embrace memories.
Whatever darkness we come to,
it is where we whisper fact.
The face is not involved.
In darkness it is possible
to comprehend the nuance of the tongue,
but it can never handle a replica.

W. POEM II
(In Memory of David Nathaniel Martin, 1907–1967)
for Joseph S. McNamara

I

The man's voice who sang
What a Friend We Have in Jesus
Was as ragged as the beginning of the Christian church.
I am not sure you would have enjoyed what I heard.
Such singing may have kept you from church.
Such moments tempt flesh and Christ.
I would deviously talk you into heaven if I could.
I came hoping that you were not dead,
That somehow we were all misinformed.
It is impossible to believe everything you hear.

II

Death is an itch, Father, we cannot properly relieve.
There is no balm to cure the annoyance.
My eye refuses to investigate your new home.
False grass and flowers decorate that yawn in the earth.
The man of cloth and collar speaks at your head.
It was 31° the day we left you to be graved.
The blanket was satin they gave you to keep warm.
They shut and folded the door at your head for the last time.

III

We leave you dishonestly lying in the wind.
Strange men you never knew and we do not know
Consign what is left of you, lumped and heavy, solemnly down.
They speak:
            of the night,
            of their wives,
            girlfriends,
            the newest whiskies,
            who makes love best,
            that you never will, again.
I know this opening earth we put you in
Will turn what is left of you into stone.

IV

It had been all the day of Thanks
Before we knew you were dead.
In a movie on Superior Street, I sat thinking:
You are not gone.
Someone plays a harpsichord.
The music almost forced me to tears.
Something squeezes the heart.
I rub the identification away like a sour taste.
Time paused in Columbus, Ohio,
struck,
Broke the pulse of your breath
And left me to build a life against our itinerant ways.

W. POEM II (A)

After we had buried you father
I bought Robt. Duncan's *Roots and Branches*
Images and sounds to soothe my conscience.
Since your going this eighth year
It all comes back, how the cold cut stark
Through to the cold in us.
Silent death brought us together
And dispersed us again.
You root, I simple branch
Have a hundred poems for leaves
Some are darker than others
Some already have withered back to first dust.
I loose my poems like young men loose their hair
Like you lost me, like mothers loose their children.
Love is so thin a muscle
That when it is finally quiet
We lay the loss in the ground
Desiring another bloom, another testament.
So heritage slips away
Like winds cascading over the body.

W. POEM III

I

My body contains the madness that is genius to my being.

II

Men of fire are like other men in the dark.
The arrow must spear straight to strike the mark.

III

O when this death is on the body Mother, and will not let it go
I search biblically for an occasional Spring woman, I would learn, I would
    know.
In my wild jungle of nerves, in the many arteries where my blood flows
That instant growth which on my skin runs from hair to toes
Is fear, a night-broken twig; courage is where the wild bird goes.

IV

O, Mother Mother yes I worry, yes I die
In all my summoning wisdom I cannot tell you why.
No answers will do now, I am confident
The fiery sun runs lover to all desperate incidents.
Mother hear, that which to you is sacred
Like women taking men to their bed
Is for me a fiction I have somewhere read.

V

I would be open with you, find some way
Like a wound when its scab peels away;
Lance the sore and drain the pus.
Ah, yes we must shape the truth, the two of us.
To speak you my truth is to recite you pain.
All is loss; nothing is gain.
I part my lips; warm breath against the cold looks like steam.
I bite into silence; I scream.
I open my eyes to a new dream.

VI

Seeing me approach forty-plus
You wonder how I feed my body's lust.
To tell you all means tears and recriminations,
Yet, these days I am more direct to the force of your questions.
Mother my personal song is no single simple thing.
No music in flight; no Messianic birds sing.
To know in what secret ways my blood moves
Is to sense the traffic, the toll, the vain accidental loves.
Love is like the highway's brief lines, push and tug, constant on my heart.
Desire is the invisible wind which tears the individual body apart
Desire is the familiar sounds that give you start.

VII

My skin gives birth to eighth notes which curl prostrate;
Age-lines mark, score, and orchestrate
This music personal, my body's long song of dissonance.
I keep close to the beat, long for the pauses, the rests, the silence.
I am wrestler, victim, challenger, and victor
Nothing can deliver me from these nightmares, this war.
I think the dead are the wisest men of all
To grant no attention to our earthly human call.
There are some secrets we would keep until after the grave
Now that I come outwardly with the truth, there is nothing to save.
So that my personal song having reached its crescendo
Must either stop or quietly diminuendo.
Between such extremes all music must go.

W. POEM IV (A)

We have said things to each other this time, Mother,
Of such minute and insignificant proportions
That my heart has been cut away from my body and slowly
Tossed into a consuming fire.
This time I am convinced
We have declared our final war
Against each other.
We will battle to the death;
Neither of us will surrender;
Something of the winner will die with each of us;
It is the way of adjustments;
The only way a victor may go on.
The tongue is a vicious instrument;
It stabs quicker than switchblade;
It does not sever discreetly,
It aims directly for the heart,
For everything in its path.
I shut off the many impulses entering my eyes.
I lock my tongue behind my teeth.
I stop when hate is too much to say.

W. POEM IV (B)

We have said things to each other this time of such vast proportions
That I felt a severing stake had been driven into my stomach,
That my heart was tied there burning slowly.
This time I am convinced
We have declared the final conflagration
We will battle to death, to defeat,
Neither will surrender;
Something of the winner will die with the loser,
It is the only way adjustments occur,
The only way the winner may go on.
The tongue is a vicious instrument,
It stabs quicker than switchblade,
It does not sever discreetly,
It aims directly for the heart
And everything in its path.
Behind my eyes, I shut off the many impulses.
Behind my teeth, I lock my tongue.
I stop when hate is too much to say.

W. POEM V
[After Philip Levine]
   for Maria Kurdi

I never praised my father
with words of water in life or death.
I write these words to you in Pecs, Hungary
knowing, in a fortnight, you will read them,
set a curious eye on my indiscriminate hand.
I am fifty-nine, watching an irritating fear
grow larger and more threatening.
I consider how faint his heart must have grown
when all his bodily functions expired at sixty.
He simply stopped on a wintry Thanksgiving evening,
somewhere in the city of Columbus, Ohio.
What had he discovered at that moment?
We buried him several days later
in a thrilling cold, in a grave that sloshed
when the coffin touched bottom.
The water must have sent another electric chill
through his already cold bones,
with an acid that ate into his flesh,
freezing each dead cell with excruciating ease.
"We cannot locate his soul anymore.
What reason can we give
for putting him in preserved stone?"
His younger sister was all reason.
When I returned to lay flowers on his sleep
I heard an old man singing in the distance,
his voice rubbed the gray stones like wind:

>   *Jesus blood never failed me,*
>   *Yet. This one thing I know*
>   *That He loves me so.*
>   *Jesus blood never failed me,*
>   *Yet.*

I ask the caretaker: "Where is X 1167?"
She points me to where my father sleeps:
"Over there in the colored folks section."

Suddenly, I am touched by the same water
which long ago ate into his flesh
regurgitated him into former clay.
Little wonder my aunt gave him,
no stone, no name, no date.
"Nothing is out there; nothing remains
when the spirit goes a-wandering," she said.
Poor father, whose love of words—
25¢ detective pulp, loose women,
and drunken Saturday nights—
led him to this place.
Standing here I wonder what
there was in his blood
that is sure to infect mine.

"My Mother never made scenes."
She was *A World of Light*
May Sarton, an act of respectability.
My Mother never made scenes.
She never failed to challenge my father
When she felt duly wronged.
Something in their angers
Always made them retreat to the bedroom,
Their disputable place of passion;
Everything was uttered under a pillow of distance,
A gray attached to their emotions.
A dark spirit moved in the rooms where we slept.
The floors knew what we could tolerate
In the evenings we laughed over whist and pitty-pat.
There was nothing to occupy the nights
When my father played solitaire.
Loneliness constantly defeated him.
Who among us could win that game
With devious slight of hand?
There was something in his blood
That would not let him surrender
Even when he could not visit
That other woman in our city
Who knew the private motions of his limbs
And could finger the mystery in his heart.
What did she know about him
That she would not reveal to my mother?
Why did the two of them never speak formally?
Now they have become faded snapshots, stills
Collected, named, dated, and boxed.

PRAYER 1

O Jesus, everyday I battle with my tender flesh
That grief, that war, that death to come
When my breath will not course my blood along.
See me, Lord, bending my knees
For my soul's salvation.
I have seen old men watch me,
I have watched younger men,
Circled them in my pupils, closed my eyelids,
And made a picture for my mind.
I go this way dreaming, Lord,
In my defective flesh.

PRAYER 2

There is an old man preaching in the streets;
His white hair tells me all his years.
The claws of eagles scrape his face.
Still he preaches a grace of blood.
He does not know the defeats I have suffered
Because the world that hangs between my legs is hungry.
No blood for this spirit; no rest for this soul;
I take my life from a wooden bowl.
A young woman leaning against her man watches and
Laughs loudly against the afternoon traffic.
This world moves with a mind of its own.

PRAYER 3

Oh, shall I not praise God
For in all my weakness I still breathe
For all my worldly loss I still see
For the errors of my ways,
Which I do not understand,
And with which I do battle everyday,
He has chosen to deliver me
Which I do not understand?

PRAYER 4

O Christ, O Christ,
I, an old man nearing forty
In *The Church of San Vitale*
Follow a boy with his girlfriend.
He has a nine-inch hard-on.
They know now that I observe them
They notice the wish in my eyes.
Their youth takes no care for such old desire.
I allow them to go away
To spend their fortunes in quiet.
I know what it means to be.

PRAYER 5
for Bernard Saftner

O specific Christ
Who knows my battles
The struggles I lose
The wars I win
In the terrain of my flesh
Where head and heart contrive
To subdue all my genital desire

O most specific Christ
I am a leaf
Falling from a tree
Caught in the wind
Between cloud and earth
Swept up   shifted down
Slowly   I touch ground
O specific Christ
Hear: my hungry voice
The words hung on my breath.
Repair my sins

PRAYER 6

In the night of the flesh
In the hell of my memory
I pastor my feelings
I shepherd my thoughts.
They are driven like sheep,
They hunger to rest
They desire to feed upon the grass,
But it is not sustenance enough.
O Jesus, O Jesus
I, who journey this hell
Surrounded by pain
Celebrate remembrance
With the blood I partake from You.

PRAYER 7
    Dearest Jesus Here Are We
    Choral Prelude
    J. S. Bach

O my Jesus
Dearest Jesus here I am
Facing my flesh
Confronting my sins
Double in pain
Triple in grief
Show me grace
Deliver me relief
Take me into that sharp country death
Where in three days
You gave birth to eternity.

PRAYER 8

O my poor derelict Jesus,
This body begs fruition,
It does not know what to do.
It turns, turns, turns for relief.
Each day I live,
Each night I sleep,
My desires are unrewarded dreams,
Nightmares assembled beneath my fingernails.

I say quiet words in my head,
O my poor derelict Jesus,
Apparel thin as whispers
Each word I breathe into my hands
Evaporates.

PRAYER 9

O Christ personal to me
My prison, my punishment, my flesh—
Prayers   words   breaths
Cartilage   bone   blood
Earth fleshly   vinegar   wood
Hold the shape of my penis
It is song that brings me close to You.

PRAYER 10

I am ceaseless like the run of blood
Splinters punish my body
Stones release my anguish
My Golgotha frozen on wood
Nerve and bone
Earth and sinew bound together.
What is the shape of blood or oxygen
Which feeds my mind?
I take deliberate refuge in Your spirit;
I exalt as I take You in.

PRAYER 11

I want to say these prayers while
I can still catch the rhythm of my pulse,
Recognize the music my breath makes.
I bend my knees, construct my prayers from steel
As if I were building a sanctuary of frame and glass.
There are no pews.
I humble myself to the ground.

PRAYER 12

Jesus
Who for all my repeated sins
They did crown Your head with thorns—
Jesus
Who for all my flesh abused
They did pierce You in the side—
Jesus
Your hands, Your feet,
Who, for my life, hammered You on this wood?
Jesus
I, who, in this flesh,
Control all my sins but one,
Hammer; I nail,
I pierce and crown You
All for my flesh abused.

PRAYER 13

You Jesus, total love,
I have heard the disciples who came after you;
I have read the prophets who came before
Still my restless soul is
Deaf as wilderness stone, silent as wild things,
Twisted like mountain trees
Shuddering like grass buried in water
Like bruised winds.
You Jesus, total Jesus,
I have listened, I understood
Still I can find no deep ground to root my human peace in.

PRAYER 14

O Jesus precious
This penitent's plea
Whose natural feet
Climbed his holy mountain
Walked the curved disposition
Of rocks, stones, and crevices,
Whose inner being seems forged
From hard steel silence,
Whose divine falling waters
Smoothed the rough ways which
Temper the insubstantial thoughts of
A spirit that deeply dwells within.

THE FORMS OF SILENCE
for Sue

I

In this the sharpest of all winters
I am considering
What we have come to mean to each other.
In the crises of wind:
I have discovered something of myself,
I comfort you and in your eyes,
Realize what flaws a glass may reveal.
I look for the details that tell all,
That plumb to the bone and beyond,
Which is the truth we seek
But do not want to see.
So this is what love is
Restless, impossible, unending,
An ulcer in the groin that bleeds,
A stomach that excommunicates,
An eye that devours all light.

The years have taught me the meaning of touch
The feel of flesh against my flesh
To challenge the thrust of thought with thought.

I have no severe complaints against the cold
These are the winds which drift with the dust of snows
That build porous mountains and cliffs
Wherein the body may sink and be lost . . .
Until summer springs in the earth
Never did I think there would be cause or time
To loose your hair pin by pin and watch
It uncurl slowly frame by frame down your back.
Whose nude did I dream you to be?
Who is the artist who has caught you in this special light?

II

Look in what a stillness
Your green plants grow.

84

Hardly, does the surrounding air move.
We do not hear them breathe.
Slowly, moment by moment,
They change ever so slightly,
And with that change,
A suddenness takes the heart.

III

Guilt devours my human sense
When I know that you are crying.
Where is my necessary compassion?
Where is my comforting speech?
It is out of single reach.
It is in a distant warring nation,
Fighting side by side with a dying that
Devours my human sense.

IV

The Act of Bricking Love

In the act of bricking love
I douse the heat of my brain
I cool the intellect in my groin
In its sublime violence
In its concentrated terror
Hoping that such a structure
Will hold against the wind
That such a measure will be full-voiced.

Let us complete our gesture together
Finalize the act, coda the music,
The architectural composition
With a sustaining veneer
Against those fortuitous years
When we are ill
When we are quietly dying.

[handwritten annotations: "building?", "Making?" near "Bricking Love"; "They want to try to work it out" next to "Let us complete our gesture together / Finalize the act, coda the music,"; "Wedding vows?" and "through sickness, Until death" near "When we are ill / When we are quietly dying."]

85

SHOWERING I

This morning I have carefully gathered the paraphernalia
With which to clean my body:
A brush to scrub away the initial dirt,
Two cloths: one face, one body,
Soap, a drying towel,
And the force of attack in my right fingers.

I enter the slender cubicle,
Turn the control counterclockwise,
Everything is covered with steam,
Even the eyes puff with water,
I soap hair, face, arms, chest,
Rough bending knees,
Forgotten elbows,
Legs, feet, and the toes between.
That is where the history of where we have been
Collects and hides.
It is in the head where things remain unjustifiable;
It is in the heart where things are truly known.
I take from my skull a thought best examined under water.

SHOWERING II

What happens sometimes
When you turn on the shower is
Too much gets washed away suddenly.
There are layers which we wish to retain,
There is also the discovery,
The coming of new layers of skin
Which amazes you that the body can still renew itself,
That as the water touches the hair
And slowly seeps to the scalp,
Even the brain begins to feel renewed,
Suddenly in the midst of water
There is a dearth of ideas not worth very much
But ideas nevertheless.
Yet if you could remember,
Salvage, wash the best of what came,
Towel it,
You might have a thought as clean as your body.

DRESSING

When I face my morning mirror
Whose definition of beauty do I see?

These marks outline my body, these define my soul;
I must be truthful with you, since I am growing old.

It is how the old people addressed themselves,
How they shaped mysteriously the will of the young,
How from the many roots of darkness
The source of their voices sprung.
Once an old black teacher said

I shall mark you with my word
Because you have not listened, not heard.
Bad, bad, evil and black,
A mighty stick shall break your mighty back.

Until you know the refutable history
There is nothing you can say.
When you have gained some knowledge
It is too late in the day.
Now that my body is refreshed,
Carefully wrapped and covered,
I descend to the extension of yesterday
To try a different route, to go another way.
I grab a piece of toast, I drink my coffee slow
I clear my throat and rush for the door.
There are no mother desires that mark my body,
No sudden eradicable fears;
I contain upon my soul the marks of sin,
The dark, unforgiven sexuality which I was conceived in.

REMEMBERING HYDE PARK

Once between Arabs and Jews,
I read poems to a passing couple
Interested in love and who wondered
That the crowds gathered to my left and right
But not close to my voice and,
That they were not moved by my words,
That no one listened,
That love was not the central issue,
That love never calls forth the crowds.
Yet, they said, "Commune with us,
Drink from our wooden cup."
I gave them in return
An offering of words.

PHONE MESSAGE FOUND ON A JOHN WALL

I ask politely to speak to you
I speak to you anonymously at first.
Your salutation is cordial.
I read your note, your name, your number
And wonder what the odds are that you exist.
You exist. I do not have to dissemble.
I say my name; I mention your message.
So truth is between us from the beginning.
I say let that always be so.

THE NEW YEAR ACCOMPLISHED

I sit among the concentric trees of the town this Sunday morning while the town bell calls its morning worshippers to its pollution-stained shires. Light is the stained glass windows between the trees. I languish in the sacred flood of this place. The grass prays; the wind hums; the earth is volatile with rejoicing this first Sunday. Tomorrow I will go out into the cornfield, among the remnants, to observe the winter damage, to see what repairs will have to be accomplished before Spring planting. This small place is like the large rings of Saturn with dust and rock debris held together by some mysterious force. The sun turns or the Earth turns and I by necessity will plow the land so that growth can begin where, in this cornfield, bounty of earth, sun, and rain fulfills the soft travail of what hand, what simple struggle, can accomplish.

MEMORY POEM FOR THE NEW YEAR
for Len Roberts

W. D. blew off three of his right-hand fingers,
Proving a worthless dare that he could hold
Firecrackers, a child's dynamite longer than anyone.
Uncle Ad declared: "Boy you have more spit
than a hound dog has ass." W. D. was left with a thumb
and an index finger with which
he could point, beckon women, and use,
in point of fact, to bring any situation to climax.
He lived into the white hair of middle-age
sauntering between furiously engaging black women
and ordinary southern white men who were
not taken in by his innate and flamboyant jive.
He only feared Nana who always threatened
to neuter him with the kitchen butcher's knife
if he didn't watch his mouth. Years later
I understood what she meant when my sweet jimmy came.
She brought his honey tongue to a stop long before
he could reach the bluster of rage and manhood.
Perhaps her single threat is what saved him
from all the white men. She held everyone
who came in that house under the pressure
of her Biblical thumb. W. D. had an easy tongue
a gracile swagger and a snaky laugh which
bounced from voluptuous neighbor woman to
neighbor woman, each of whom dreamed of the
taste of his bright spangle. He said:
"They all love me Nana; I can't keep
them away. I can see the desire,
like a thin hot flame, flickering
somewhere in their contrived dark."
How hard it must have been for him
to keep them all within desirable range.
In the shadow, he trained Cousin Billy
in the art of his deft and clever maneuvers;
I longed to follow them blocks away from home,

to learn the escapades of their secret ways.
There would never be scissors strong or sharp
enough to cut the threads of Nana's voice.
She had watched liquor and sex suck in
the men around her; I was not to be lost.
She would bring one of us to salvation
if she had any say.

THE COLORED SECTION OF THE THEATRE

neglected because the colored section doesn't exist anymore.

for James and Linda Chervenka

I have climbed up the wooden stairs beyond where the Italian marble left off,
high above everything else where only birds can breathe,
in the thin and frayed air.
I am led by a friend who has felt the same presence of humans who once sat
in these seats and wants me to feel it too.
I hear the haunted rattle in their voices.
The laughter is stale; the applause inaudible.
The light is muted here; the dust has taken years to settle.
The old footsteps are muffled;
the extra dust seals the weathered cracks in the floor.
Rejection hangs musty in this place.
Far below on the human stage, the actors are small-boned birds.
Their words and gestures float up like well-turned batter;
every smooth vowel to be tasted, smelled.

HERE
for Linda and Jim

Beyond the point where the exquisite marble left off,
The wooden stairs in this old theatre have become
So narrow that only one body may pass.
High above everything, only birds can speak.
The air here is thin as frayed linens.
A friend wants to introduce me to
The silk presence she has felt.
She has watched the dust flicker on these benches.
I listen for the same sacred rattle,
For echoes of laughter gone stale,
Of applause so old the bones crack.
Light is muted here,
Ancient horrors in the settled dust.
It patches the worn floors
Where rejection hung like old humidity
Unable to evaporate. Here old neglect   *the title. the theater is neglected*
Lies covered under a thin membrane of dust
Waiting for the clean chance to infect again.

THE SPOILS OF THE DAY

At the end of my palm there were five blind avenues and
four invisible spacious routes leading to the weekend
picture show when I was ten and wealthy enough to sustain
a bus ride, stage show, two full-length features, a serial,
popcorn, and sometimes candy, and if I was early enough
on Friday nights, I could see the entire event twice:
Hopalong Cassidy, Roy Rogers, Gene Autry chasing the bad guys,
like useless herds, over cliffs on into the Pacific so that
the good people of the world might have seven days of contemplation.
That was the bonus for being good
and I could still make it home by eleven o'clock.
Mama was lenient when the house was prosperous.
When our hopes were veiled or thwarted in frustration
I had to be earlier than early.
No use adding worry to unnecessary burden.
When things were O. K. at the corral I could see the Movietone News
which always made me shudder tears at real life
especially when they excavated the bodies of dead jews.
What sour cruelty.
Those souls did not escape the traps set for them by smiling villains
of Nazi Germany. No twelve or thirteen chapters for the maligned.
No white ten-gallon hat Autry, Cassidy, or Rogers winning in the end
Or listening to our black cheers of liberation.
This was a sweet horror I was too young to understand,
and yet I knew, in my bones, these people should not be dead.
No hero appeared even at the last minute to save the incinerated bones.
All the evidence went up in untraceable smoke.
The horror of such a crime grew in my imagination
as I made my way home after the moving pictures.
I alone am privy to the fact that the heroes or heroines did not get there
    in time;
I am not happy with my licensed information about serial outcomes.
I would be happier if someone else had seen the spoils of that day.

SASSY MUSIC

The tree is alive with sassy music.
The crickets in the ground grasses
maintain a rough continuo;
they have the spirit power of a
Dies irae, dies irae whose premonition
is not about love or sacrifice
but of hedonist Eve who wanted
every bit of gossip about Eden
which has been the exegesis
of every priest, mullah, rabbi who
possesses a functioning esophagus
offering grace and redemption
as high as a raging falsetto
of Southern black, white
Protestant preachers who
know, without question, that
the overreaching unifier
is the suffering Christ.
Then they turn to the
Offertory which is
the Pentecost of
every religious house
of love in the making.
Each practitioner
is asked to join
in the kindness of
delicious and enthralling
giving, a kind of
somnolence of being
where you end up
giving away the self
before the final amen.
Charity, repent,
Pusillanimous strength
are the musts
to instigate rapture
which led to the

inevitable carnage of Carthage.
The voices of heaven
rejoiced with celestial song
all a façade filled with dark passion
a tradition the community hailed with petty
relationships of dear heart peace thoroughly
grazed with sunshine quiet and friendship family.
Money is a fine precipice from which to jump.
Each believer is called to deliver faith insatiable.

IN MEMORY OF ETHERIDGE KNIGHT
(1931–1991)

Death walked up close to me
Through the mud and mines of Korea.
His voice became my white prison;
his touch my exquisite fear.
So when the doctors approached
with that medicinal air which
prevents them from speaking truth,
I demanded nothing less. They said:
"You are terminal, Mr. Knight."
I replied, "I came here with that fact
slapped indelibly on my ass."
Words are sharp like a surgeon's knife
cutting near the bone of diagnosis;
they must be as invasive as this cancer
which has the morals of a rapist.
My grandmother's words
rounded the corners of her wisdom.
She kept faithful records of the living,
the dead, and the missing.
My words are chosen like her gait,
a century old and careful,
the strut of woman, the smile of promise.
We go down as we come up.
Our ancestral shine is all that matters.

OUT OF THE DEAD BONES
for Tamas Juhasz

Out of the dead bones, out of the shaled dust,
Where one lovely and ordinary mammoth lays down
Its heavy flesh, in this secret place, having
Been driven here by the trumpet of a violet
Whose voice was thrust out upon waves of heat.
This place of death no poacher's greed may claim.
Only the African sun knows where the residue
Of bodily wealth lies. The night is the last guard
Before coming upon the startling bones and tusk
Which remain here. All their bulk has disappeared
Like the heavy gases from a jet stream strung from
Prague to Sierra Leone, like the shadowed stripes
Slowly disappearing from a shaman's robe.
The ribs are the parentheses of what once was,
For these zigzag deaths are tightly wrapped
In veils no human eyes may unwrap or discover
The mammoth in its final and amazingly sweet anguish.

THE SERENDIPITOUS CAT

There was once a serendipitous cat
who always walked with a cornstalk cane,
who went home every evening to watch his
lovely macaroni wife, all starch
and wonderful. She met him every
evening with the soft words "Bon Soir"
which wrapped around the root of his being;
how velvet and seductive those words were.
They were an invitation written on silk parchment.
He knew what the words meant and never hesitated
once he had been invited. He always expected to see
his wife in the doorway first.
He was prepared to make a smooth entrance,
to embrace the sweet red of her breath
which enveloped him like exhausted heat.
The message which inevitably came across
the wire found him alert
and listening to her words and ready
to follow their slightest suggestion.
Such words, as they were, led him
toward the precipice of space,
for whatever it was that she uttered,
in the silk dark, never failed to dazzle.

GINKGO TREES

The ginkgo trees publicly
Undressed themselves yesterday;
Their leaves slipped down
The flesh of the air
Like bright yellow negligees
Tickling the afternoon.
We quilt ourselves
In that seductive loveliness.

TIGHT ROPE WALKING THE AIR

three pairs of jordan sneakers
(primed for flight,
rich with wear,
able to shield
some winter feet
against the day)
dangle like electricity
laces of carbon wire
a dali painting
all surreal in the autumn air.

MY MOTHER AT THE END OF HER DAYS

My mother at the end of her days could not see to sign
Her name on the dotted line. She could write her name;
It was the line that caused trouble. She had a sweet name;
I cannot deny. So many communal ancestors died trying
To learn how to write. How could impatient haste deny
Her the opportunity to honor those dead she would soon
Face? I was not the best counselor in those failing days.
Time for the Banker was golden and mighty, still he
Could not afford her the time it took to place her name
On the dotted line the Law required. She was forced
To set down Slavery's strong X. With those two improper
Strokes all of her joys were denied. I wept that that
Act set a longing in her heart and took from her hand
An accomplished task, she had learned long ago.
I am far from that clinical day
And the impolite act I was forced to commit against
A love removed and dying aggressively of cancer.

YOU SHALL SKIP THROUGH THIS MUSEUM: LIFE

for Carl and Kathe Kothemier

I
Miro, husband
a patient young man in a red tam,
with long blonde hair and beard,
teaches his pupils all he knows
of your world, your childhood fantasies
where everything is possible,
with lights and explosions,
dreams and snakes, stars and water,
and the body full of childhood distortions,
as you have imagined them.
A world of dragons,
lightning and smoke
that appears from nowhere
and just as quickly goes back to nowhere.
It is a world where you can walk upright
or walk upside down.
It is the universe we inhabit
before we are born.

II
The red moon is imprisoned
in the place where the heart takes residence.
The colors open as suddenly
as a woman with the face of the moon.
(deceased wife)

III daughter life
A little girl skips through this museum
around the people who look at the etchings.
She understands best this carnival:
of juggling objects, a twirling rope,
the flying trapeze, the ball dancer,
of exploring the world in a drop of water.
The teacher's students will make their reproductions.
They have the best understanding of love in their fingers.

TEN VARIATIONS ON A WALK

for Harry and Catherine Rougier

0.

When I open my door to look out
The cold rushes in.
I trudge single into the night.

I.

In a park,
Cold as night,
Dark as the depth of stone,
Hollow as an empty bone.
Two lovers sit.
Their tongues embrace.
Only the snow and I move.

II.

The cold dives into the skin.
The two lovers remain together in the park
I walk upon dead snow.
My wandering feet know where to go.
Beneath a still incandescent light,
Only I and the snow move.

III.

Sunday morning.
I repeat Saturday's steps.
The snow has paused.
Light barters for day.
A squirrel scurries before me.
I shade my eyes against
The approaching sun.
There is no hiding from the wind.

IV.
The cold wind turns a leaf
Huge   dervish
Turn   wild circle
Totentanz
Invisible madness
Wind   settles
A stillness presides.

V.
The shape of a memory is:
A cold wind,
An exquisite snowflake,
Two quiet lovers.

VI.
The mouth is a passion,
A warm comfort,
A place that utters agony,
A place that utters song.

VII.
What is there about the cold
That stills the moving blood
That suggests the foot take caution
When it walks upon ice?

VIII.
Look there
Through the
Icy air
Where those
Lovers make
A warm pair,
Flesh and heart,
Sighs and starts.
Quickly can you
Read the words
On their breaths?

IX.
When I am done with
This morning's walk
I return to my private dwelling.
When I am inside, I listen to the street
Outside echo the stale snow.

RETURN FROM WALKING

I.

I have returned to the city
Where half my disasters reigned.
It has rained here these past three weeks.
The common complaint is: the scientists
Have put too many holes in the sky,
That real place we go when we expire.
In our persistence there must be
Another way to explore the moon.

II.

In the back alleys of the world,
Freely, I have taken love,
I have found new pleasures
In deep midnight.
The souls I wandered for,
The groins I hungered after,
The groins that hungered after me,
May be cause for laughter,
But half the world I've seen
Has this terrible need,
This interminable desire.

III.

I stand, watch, and wait,
Like all the other men
Who sometime beg,
Who sometime give up.
We, who grant favors,
Who receive them, take
What we can knowing
Half the world is filled with pain,
Half the world walks with grief.
I know how to speak the truth
And that these words bring no relief.
I have taken the rose from the bush,

The thorn from the stem,
The petal from the bulb.
I know to cruise is
To walk and walk and walk.

THE OLD GRAVES

From where I go to work these days
I look out and see the old graves,
The ones that relatives have long since
Placed besides obsolete figures in their memory,
And the new ones which are quick in the survivor's brain.
I must teach the old graves that there is
Something sacred in the memory.

QUIETLY, QUIETLY, THEY REMEMBERED THOSE WHO DIED

Quietly, a thousand men marched
To the town's monument for the dead,
And left wreaths and small sprays to their memory.
No traffic disturbed their walk.
The footsteps seemed to make no noise.

There were four men crucified in stone,
They stood for the town's heroes:
Two to the left of the man in the center,
And one to his right.
They are guarded by wolves
Who howl and snarl their personal pain.

O, memory, memory what is this passing stone
That the wind gnaws upon?

WHEN YOU ARE OLD ENOUGH

When you are old enough and tired
You will begin to seek God
In His houses.
There you will find
Quiet sanctuary
From this world's rush.
See there:
An old woman comes with a rose.
An old man comes with withered hands.
They will lay their gifts down
To keep a solid promise.
A man's years are like the seasons.
A woman's years are like the Spring.

POEM

There is an old man walking alone.
He sees something distinctly invisible beside him.
He dismisses it with a wave of the hand,
With words I am too far away to hear.
He turns the corner into another way.
The wind and sun go with him;
His age is enough to command.

WALKING THE OLD GROUND

This morning I walked the old ground
That we had walked together
Where the night held the silence
Like we held our breaths
Like we made love
Touched and turned
With the night
That held the silence.
Light invades;
A birdsong follows.
The day holds a different history.
This morning weds you to my memory.

QUIETLY

I woke up this morning,
Looked at you sleeping next to me.
In the bathroom the electric light
Cut between me and my mirrored image.
I relieved myself, showered,
And as I washed, I thought: of last night,
Of our struggling in the grip of love,
Of our winning the struggle,
Of our relaxing
Triumphant.
Immediately, I rinsed the soap away,
Returned to bed
And touched you.
Quietly.

DAWN

As the dawn edges
Over this cool morning
A gathering of common sparrows
Splashes, busy flutter in water:
Fallen rain in a pool
By the side of the road.
Suddenly a speeding car:
Dispersal . . . flight . . . silence.
The dawn edges on.

DÜRER
for Neal and Melinda

It is the fury that he placed between arteries and veins.
It is what he understood about touch, grasp, point, and feel.
It is all there. After you pass grief, you come to quiet;
You pleasure awhile in the love of:
A woman in the arms of a man,
The two holding hands, or
The man running his finger along the arm of the woman.
Behind such pleasure there is a wish no other wish can match.
We small men who would take the earth in our hands,
The air in our bodies, must risk the terrible fury of water
And the craving sacrifice of fire.

A NEGRO SOLDIER'S VIET NAM DIARY

The day he discovered a mother and child in the river, he wrote:
They had been there a month; the water had begun to tear them apart.
The mother had not relaxed; even in death she held to her child.
I lowered my gun into the water, walked away.
My stomach screamed empty, there was nothing there.
What little warm water I had would not Pilate away the mud or stench.
It was like a dead body we could not discover.
Death hangs on the rice.
The ground is watered with blood.
The land bears no fruit.
Grass is an amenity.
It is a luxury to notice so much as a flower
Or clear water in a stream.
Bullets here kill with the same deliberate speed that they do at home.
Fear destroys the thing it is unacquainted with.
I never want to kill again.
Do not celebrate me when and if I come home.
I step around the smallest creatures these days.
I am cautious to pray.
I am cautious to believe the day will come when we can
Take up our sharing again with deliberate speed.
Have you prayed, lately, for that?

OF LOVE, OF WAR

They tarred and feathered a girl in Ulster the other day.
They say the cause was a British Army Man, O!
They say the cause was love.
In times of war reserve your love, the old ladies warned.
In times of love reserve your war.
They tarred and feathered a girl in Ulster the other day.
They say the cause was love, O?

O SAMURAI
  for Yukio Mishima

He let go of life with courage,
Fed his blood to the snow.
Everything it touched turned perfect red.
When the wind swept away that winter
The crust of his life softened the earth.

DEATH IS A DEPARTURE IN LOVE
for Daniel

I am patiently waiting for you to leave,
Like the day I came home from town
And the neighborhood kids wanted to be
The first to tell me Cousin Louise had died.
They all ran to me and said,
Your grandmother is dead.
Some of them confused their lines.
They argued the truth; I didn't believe them.
So I ran home in ignorance.
It was true; she was gone.
Mary E. Strong would undertake her body.
The bed clothing had been removed,
The mattress was being aired,
The frame was dismantled and washed.
The room was emptied of everything.
How quickly cleaning confirms death.
So when you are gone, Friend,
I shall vacuum the room,
Rearrange the desk and bed,
Scrub all the places you have touched,
Sit Shiva,
Close that period in my life
And never   never   look back.

MOURNING WORDS FOR MURDER BY ONE'S OWN HAND
for Freddie Prinze

I remember the humor that flirted
On the landscape of your tongue.
There is, in this studio, the need
The terrible need to speak
Out against silence,
A longing to utter some final
And lasting sentence
To the kingdom of grass,
To the place of revealing waters.
There is a touch and comfort in the air
That settles on the ear like music
That seduces the heart effectively.

Time which sought you painfully
Was the muscle and population of your mind.
The passion of flesh and death
Which could not alleviate you
From the kleigs that seared every vein,
Whose heat dried up your every emotion.

Our anger ravages the space we speak into;
We set fire to the air we touch.
O Friend, even the air is outraged
Because it must, with final duty, creep beneath
Corrupted age and decay no matter
What we have dreamed as possible.

SESTINA: LINES TO AN UNKNOWN SUICIDE

They speak vicariously of your personal history
That you took a gun in your hand and pulled its spring,
Allowed a single bullet, in your brain, free access
Through its rigid and confined corridor
To absent you from foe: new, old, close, far,
To set you steady, on a course, to the nearest star.

They picked up your body like a fallen star,
Bound it to a stretcher. That's history.
After midnight nothing seems far,
Except the warm and longed-for spring.
They rolled you down a path that seemed a corridor
With only north and south as its access.

They took you away; now, no one has access
To you. Do you wander like the light of a familiar star
Infinitely down the sky, space's only corridor?
In some deep and private way I touch your history.
Time has advanced beyond the end of that spring.
Where is your mature spirit; has it gone far?

Some pains punish, others drift with nature far.
Was there no other route, no immediate access,
No promise upon which you might spring?
What is the brilliance of a perceived star?
I am intrigued by your brief history.
I touch your despair in this corridor.

Your friends were greeted with your death in this corridor.
Between the distance and the act, knowledge is never far.
So rapid is the moment of history
That no matter what one thinks, all is access.
I say light is the best way to achieve a star.
What shall we do now with the coming spring?

We shall have to begin anew; we shall spring
From our severed memories confined in this corridor.

Light is the only way to perceive a star.
Truth is the only other access,
Whose length of years seems extreme, far,
But so is grace, the liquor of excess and history.

This winter's history is still what we take to spring.
There is no true access to freedom through this corridor,
It is tedious and far; we must take guidance from any star.

BALLAD OF A FIRE

In eighteen hundred and forty-five
There was a fire insidiously alive.
How it began, how it started, no one knows;
Fact disappears the older it grows.

Some say it was the washerwoman's fire:
A sudden wind, a sweeping momentary air.
How it began, how it started, no one knows;
Truth disappears the older it grows.

Some looked for the cause at the end of town
Among the visiting circus, the fire-carrying clowns.
How it started, how it began, no one knows;
Joy disappears the older it grows.

Some alluded to the local blacksmith's shop.
Did it start there? Did it stop?
How it began, how it started, no one knows;
Quality disappears the older it grows.

That was a town so full of life,
In a rapid hour it burned to grief.
Why it began, why it started, no one knows;
Progress disappears the older it grows.

From Diamond to Wood to Water Street
Fear was the presence Caution would meet.
When it began, when it started, no one knows;
Patience disappears the older it grows.

The tragedies were certain; they tallied the toll:
Men, women, the children in the wooded knoll.
How it began, how it started, no one knows;
Love disappears the older it grows.

In that area where the men met in prayer,
There was a holocaust of suffocating air.
What began it, what started it, no one knows;
Faith disappears the older it grows.

When evening came there was no one at all;
Even Justice reputedly fled the City Hall.
How it began, how it started, no one knows;
Courage disappears the older it grows.

Now, that town lies devastated in its dream;
Pain and Ruin, disastrously, stalk supreme.
When it ended, the exact time everyone knows;
Myth is the only offspring of the rose.

BALLAD

Waste not all your youth on study
Nor give it all to frivolity.
I have come some years to forty,
Take my eyes and see.

All that the body's constitution serves
Inches closer and closer to the grave.
For my generation and their nerves
There is nothing they can save.

Take some care for lying in the summer grass.
Make your house from the hardest stone.
Beware! A brick will trip the unsure foot;
Observe it can break a bone.

Take water, take wine, work the earth,
Eat bread, feel the warmth in a flame.
Every man has but one birth,
Find the purest marble and inscribe your name.

SONNET: WATCH HOW A BIRD FLIES
for Louis and Katyun Marre

If I should preach to you the gospel of the word,
Intone even the liturgy of the slightest syllable,
Know that they must be tasted, in part heard
And joined to that line which calls the faithful.

From all feeling, faith proceeds from the heart.
The brain aims for balance, pares away the false,
It slivers and smoothes each idea; each start
Controls the rhythm so there is no dross.

Where is that music the old poets sang?
How did they tune those melodies so fine,
And never once leave a caesura hang?
They measured strictly all their love with time.

To explain the sonnet is difficult
Watch how a bird flies, with ease; exalt.

SONNET: THE EXPENSE OF MEMORY

That month, that September, everything was memory.
I woke one morning with dreams in my eyes
Took the road away from those solitary
Fears, from that prison where the heart resides.
Those many years are past. I piece together
Sure courage and choose what feelings I have left.
I quilt memories into a new craft.
Contentiously, I stitch my sweet thoughts.
The way I hem and design there is no
Disguise. Simply, your love was thread taut.
So my faults were real; mine, the greed to know.
The course, the choice they all seemed to be right;
I exchanged love's values for private night.

ONCE THERE WAS A STONED FOX
for Kathy Williamson

who
caught
men
individual
between
a
few
words
and
the
single
moves
of
her
body.
Those
who
considered
themselves
lucky
ever
after
lived
happily
only
for
that
moment.

MOSES
for Robert Hayden

(vocal representative of
that God who spoke in fire,
who was heard in the wind,
who descended from the mountaintop
with his objections etched in stone)
now sits as if Judgment were come.
He holds the tablet he once broke in his right arm.
His left hand rests stately on his stomach.
He fingers his beard that tells us he is old,
but his muscles tell us he is as young
as when he faced the Pharaoh
or that sea which deepened itself
with the men it swallowed,
or when he chastised those tribes
dancing worship to the golden calf.
He looks, eternally, as if he is listening
to God whispering.

WHISKEY IS A PARADOX

I saw a man
forty years before his end
drive his wife like a nail into her coffin.
These will appear as ordinary comments
about his blackness:
his acquaintance with rats
whose necks he trapped for that wife,
or in his stupor called on God to damn
the clever ones who escaped prisons like his own.
His was an attitude conditioned early,
knowing there will be no night's rest
when his bed is as hard as winter earth.
He made whiskey his paradox and attempted to dream.

I SING OF AN EARTH THAT IS YET ASTONISHING

I sing with a human voice to simplify nature
I sing you a place of warmth
Of an earth that is astonishing yet
What you take from the stars is light that transports cool
What you take from the wind you shall give back in touch
What you take from the moon you shall give back as water
What you drink from the river you shall enjoy as life
What yield you harvest from the autumn earth you shall share
And when the land freezes you shall walk with caution on ice
What you take from the snow, give again in warmth
When you breathe spring, know it is the breath of love
Learn to sing as exotic men do

SIX VARIATIONS ON THE THEME OF RAIN

0
The rain
falls
slowly
and not
too hard.

1
The rain
falls
slowly.
Rain
long as
worms falls
as lightly.

2
Rain
falls
slowly
long
as
worms
falls
as
lightly.

3
Rain
lightly
falls
long
as
worms.

4
The
rain

worms
its
way
through
air
and
earth.

5
Cold
melted
ice
falls
quietly
upon
the
ground
sometimes
the wind
throws
the pieces
against the
window.
Does the
wind want
to come
in or
for me
to simply
be his lover?

SNOW
for Sarah

When great clouds fall on my tongue
The heat there destroys them.
The taste is bland;
There are no exotic seasonings.
I inhale in rapid succession
A million pounds of air.
My body rises swiftly
I fill the sky;
I absorb earth water;
I float marvelously away.
The wind and I race until we are exhausted.
We rise so high we are unseen.
I grow heavy with years;
The wind cannot sustain me.
I am an enormous cloud;
I fall in thin pieces,
Reassemble myself upon the ground.
I preserve myself with water;
I weigh myself down.
I am a solid blanket filled with stars.

NOVEMBER 1
for my Fall 1973 students

All night long
The rain and wind
Celebrate
Their marriage.
Sometime,
In the night,
The wind boldly
Opened my door
And came in.
The rain refused to follow
And went its solitary way.

This morning the wind
Scurries over the heads of grass,
Shakes the Queen Anne's Lace,
Climbs through a lone and small tree.
The sun comes offering consolation
But the wind runs on
Looking for the rain.

NOVEMBER 2

for John Suppnick

The rain came back last night,
But the wind had slipped among the blank trees.
They held among them the stare of sorrow.
The rain left traces like mirrors.
Grief drives the wind like a plague.

NOVEMBER 3

Leonard, today
I heard Phyllis's voice in a bookstore
Where I was browsing. It was that same
Heavy laughter she always shook with.
Fear took me by the shoulders,
Turned me to see, but she was not there.
In her place some other woman stood,
I did not know her.
Coldly, I remembered
Death came for her second.
When he intrudes that way
You try to speak the mind
As clearly as you feel.

ADDRESS TO MR. CHARLIE
for Le Roi Jones

I have watched you murder my people and said nothing.
I have watched you incarcerate them and said nothing.
I have watched you sentence them to rooms of filth.

I have heard you dealing in words.
I observe the sound of your speech.
I learn the subtleties you teach.
I am Shylock in black skin.
You have taught me revenge.
I understand the lessons.

I have seen the dogs bite my people.
I have watched you billy their mind's pride.
I have seen them madly marched to wars
To defend a democracy they cannot share.
I have bit my tongue patient.
Speak me no heaven.
What is, is now.
Unshackle my time and flesh!
If towns burn
              We have watched you burn them
If you are mercilessly killed
              We have watched you kill
If we smile in your eye
              You have taught the smile
We learned the lessons
              We are the masters, now.
If men shut their doors against fear
              It is because you have burned the crosses
              It is because you have murdered the night
If there is no music in the land
              It is because you have interrupted the rhythm.

I DREAM YOU HARLEM
for Adam Clayton Powell

I dream you Harlem in a single American town
Where the simplest child, spider-webbed in Negro hallways
Is not deceived by democracies of love.
Where they are broke lightning from
The ordinary mothering string, and the old . . .
The old sit withered in their passive bones
As the major star dries them in frames of age.
Because I dream you Harlem do not be deceived.
Men break love harder than rock, fish, or water.
Children unable to dream remain conditional.
Stones do not swim; fish do not walk;
Water maintains the state of insistence.
In common towns Harlem, there are a thousand
Rooms of despondencies no one remembers
Being passive in their bones.
I dream you main Harlem, as a child
Going with pearl eyes, desiring
In a folly of wind to breathe the air purely.
The filament in the hallway pierces plumb.
Bleak as an inexpensive fix, it lights the way
For a child who whines for what is not there,
Who weeps that a rat has eaten away his sister's heart,
That the bedbug drinks his blood without restraint,
And the cockroach is able to feed upon morsels
Too small to satisfy his thin human hunger.
Do not be deceived Harlem,
Though these dreams be single to my sleeping.

THE EXORCISM

Before I leave this town
There is one thing you ought to know.
The first time I said I loved you
I was as honest as the summer's warm.
In a manner of speaking, that's crazy man's talk.
What other way does a man bleed the full moon without seeming foolish?
He acts.
If a man follows his heart the journey is difficult.
The fool that watches what he eats is wise.
I didn't bring you no flowers.
Didn't come to say goodbye with no gold.
Woman, on your rough road I grew old,
Lost years like few men ever do.
My ache all come from loving you;
It all come from loving you.
I ain't going to associate with no white gal,
I ain't going to associate with no black gal,
Don't you think no red or yellow one will do neither.
You women are all the same!
Vanity is your game.
That's the first thing I'm going to tell you for a change!
Next I'm going to look in the mirror and see myself fine!
Get me some fine black walks, some slender zippers,
And some bright buttons, then I'm going to exhibit.
I'm going to get in all the windows for you to look at.
Let you drool; wag your greedy tongue;
Lick your red lips, roll your eyes,
Then let the window dresser pull the drapes
Because my price is too high.

THE LADY HAS HER SAY
for Joan Geurin

Listen to me Woolworth Man.
Who you think needs a store-bought boy
That's got a price tag on his leg?
Who you think is anxious to possess a pretty toy?
Me? Huh! Your thinking is mighty wrong.
I want a real strong man with life in his craw:
Who understands what it takes to give
Who feels the pulse to live,
Who can generate heat all through my house
'Cause I'm a sweet meat mama
That don't do nobody crying,
That refuses to spend time lying,
And don't have to waste no time trying,
'Cause my strawberries are plump and red
And sweet throughout.
So go right ahead;
Take a train,
Fly a plane,
Hop in a car,
Double, triple the distance
Make it four times as far.
Don't hesitate for my sake
Store-bought man,
I got you at the five and dime.

GRAND CENTRAL STATION

The sounds
The madness of it all again
The people who make passage here
Give off a certain warmth,
But the building is cold.
Its function is to facilitate
The "cross roads of the nation."
We make ceremony from all sorts of occasions.

I have been standing here for forty-five minutes
I am not sure that you are here
You are not sure that I am here
Or that I will ever arrive.
No one is ever sure of the promises he makes.

We may both be circling the pagoda of information
Missing each other like comic instances.
That is the way occasions are.
We cross paths, parallel bodies,
Learn the departure of trains in seconds
And in single instances we decide.
No one is ever sure of the promises he makes;
We make ceremony from all sorts of occasions.

SAFE AND SOUND

The old grandmother took special care to warn him.
She said: "At the end of every school year the young
Boys are horny. Be careful. There are dark dangers
Out there, and no one knows where they come from.
They work slowly; they take a long time to kill you.
The agony is unimaginable. Mrs. Francine's son
Died of it awhile back. I watched her nurse him until
There wasn't much left of him or her. It took away
Every ounce of her strength, yes it did. I have to say
She met the task head on, with grace I'd say. He was
Home; he was her care. So boy, when you are out
There experimenting, as you young people like to
Call it, be careful; watch where you go, watch who
You go with, watch what you do and especially
What you drink. I know I can't stop you but it is my job
To tell you things happen. Our emotions get the better of us
And we give in, and sometimes we sin. It is our helpless
Nature. But remember the Lord forgives if we are truly
Repentant. That's what *The Holy Bible* says. So you listen,
Carefully, to your teachers this school year. Learn as much
As you can about this old terrible world and you come home
Safe and sound to me."
"Yes Ma'am," he said.

DARK PRONOUNCEMENTS

Old Miss Molten was preacherly black. She could curse her students
with her left eye, while her right eye proceeded with the business
of roll calling. You knew, at once, you would never recover from
the curse of that left eye or stem the tide of its powers. This was
more than suggested fear. It all came true, especially if she took a
mind to voice a specific opinion about your future. Her tongue was
full of terrible possibilities; her tongue knew all the dark
assurances. So when my time came, and it did, she warned me fully
that: "You will never succeed without Maurice; he is your worldly
insurance against failure."

So, here I am years later trying to function alone, fighting an
average existence, not knowing which direction Maurice took for his
life, because in our youth, we lost touch with each other, and as
we moved on our separate ways, I realized that moving eradicates as
imperceptively as a sudden snow fall. Soon you forget that promise
to write, or discover you have no forwarding address to send your
regulated thoughts to. The rest becomes a memory that takes up
formal residence behind the eyes.

My mother who was, equally, never at a loss for astonishing metaphor
said to me with the same dark clarity of a curse: "You will, for all
intents and purposes, end up shitting and stepping in it. You will
need an expert recipe for cleaning the scent from your shoes."

It is amazing to me now, how those two voices merged layer upon layer
like the skin of my life. I step with caution, and try to avoid the
thick tongue of truth. I glide my feet along true and necessary
longitudes: the perimeters of stone, wood, and old macadams.
I realize it is not mere luck or chance that Maurice and I do not touch paths
any longer. Our boyhoods cannot be assessed by a reasoned brain. What
does the brain know of curses? I try to stand clear of the gray
prophesies of old women, and practice friendship within close
proximity of what the human hands can accomplish.

PLAYING UNTIL FORGETFULNESS COMES
for James and Barbara Farrelly

"Remember all the things I have said," then mama went to work. Summer Mondays are timeless in the hands of boys. The older family men harbored nothing but tedium and black failure moving in their veins. Who in society had ever permitted them to feel one eventful day? I know the answer for the men in my family; I watched each of them die of ignorant neglect. I cannot tell you how many times I watched a soft-liquor thirst take over one of their bodies and ravage its spirit of decency on that first Monday of the month when the "Sick and Accident" had to be paid. The insurance money was always hung in its envelope behind the photograph of Jesus. So we knew where to go when the insurance man said "Collect." One of those troubled Mondays Uncle Ad reached behind salvation and removed the protective policy. They took that reserved money to the local beer garden and traded health and caution for Jack Daniels. It is still astonishing to me how that money could have disappeared from behind the family savior without my knowledge. There are always slights of hand that no one can perceive. When mama came home from work and discovered that money gone, she screamed so loud a chill went through the bones of that house. "You were not mindful of what I said. You were playing instead. Somebody, somebody was in the house. No kids are supposed to be in this house when I am at work. How many times do I have to tell you? So who did you have in here playing? Don't lie to me today; I'm too tired! Do you know how many hours it took me to earn that much money just to stay a step ahead of that old insurance man? That was all the extra money I had this month. He's always at the door when I ain't got no money, and the one time I'm prepared to meet him face to face, you go and let some sorry-assed kid in the house who steals me blind. Go on, get out of my sight before I beat you both to death." Well when she was calm and finished crying, our next door neighbor, who kept her eyes on everything which happened in the neighborhood, said: "Helen those kids didn't do nothing wrong. They did just what you told them to. It was the men. I seen them quietly leave out the back way while the kids were in the front playing and soon they came back with a brown bag under your uncle's arm, and just before the insurance man came they left again by the back door staggering like Cooter Brown. Well I know drunk when I sees it, and that was drunk. Those kids don't know when the men got that money and were gone. There is no need to punish them or the air. They're not the guilty ones." Well I tell you we could have used mama for the insurance money. She was sorry as sorry could be all over the place. First we didn't know how to calm her raging arms; then we didn't have the power to release her prayerful sorrow. Still we knew that with time she would regain her innocent and unlimited supply of forgiveness and love.

APPROACHING THE NEW YEAR IN PECS
for Laszlo Komlosi

The city children bleed the old woman with sweet horns;
They herald the New Year. She sifts through throwaways
That no longer merit love. Cherry bombs curse her skin;
A celebration, a rash, a sudden texture on her body. She
Makes no discoveries, no wastes of bread, no wine left
To be drunk. She looks with devastating concentration; her
Eyes flash old disturbances. She pleads with her innocent
Tormentors. Her complaints are filled with pleasure; the
Young boys take no heed; the young girls convulse with
Laughter. The adults pursue their own ways; women greet
Death as if it were the old year; men begin to mourn the
New in their *palacksor*. They greet and kiss old friends
Naturally. One woman with a voluptuous heart loves
Every male citizen. They bless her with bountiful kisses.
Her elder is driven by the lust of necessity. She braces
Herself against the particular cold; she moves carefully
In her dread coat, felt hat, and attached purse. She is the
Lady exquisite in public. Her principal days are gone.
Fury is her excuse for rummaging the local trash cans.
The sound of anticipation is an ache in her spine; her
Ears are infected with old reminders, remote dignities
Of another time. An attentive father stands between
The old woman and her hunger. She is unsettled motion.
The air does not spell out her anger clearly. Her fading
Esteem haunts the father; she is too far gone, he cannot
Rescue her from madness. He watches her conversing
With the violet wind and knows there are no more days
Of ease for her.

THE WASHERWOMAN'S FIRE

My immigrant mother cooked her white clothes alive.
From dawn to five she boiled them, turned them over,
Then removed them and said, "You must whip the dirt
From your clothes if you want them to be clean."
Then she rinsed them twice and hung them to dry facing
Southtown. There were shirts, sheets, and pillowcases;
Ruffles, ties, silks, and laces. Every Monday morning
My father built her iron pot a fire, then filled it with
Water. Carrying water is a tall command for a small daughter.
The fire seemed always there, so did the pot. On my natal day,
June 6, 1845, a spark reached beyond that pot and caught a ride
On a derelict piece of paper. It was a hungry wind which carried
That torch like a human passion. It stirred the entire community.
It left a trail as it began to eat the dry grasses and then the wood
Frames that shaped the houses; soon Southtown was all aflame.
The fire was sudden, quick, abiding. It grew to full life in an hour.
From Diamond to Wood to Water Street, smoke and wind swept
Fear into every heart. The losses were certain; the deaths
Tallied and assured. A lunching wind, an enormous fireball,
Swirled around a fireman and burned him through to the blood.
A delicate woman who refused to leave her home knelt down
In a private place, and all that was left was a gathering of bones
Fused together. When the evening came, the fire settled gently.
The cinders smoldered. Now when I have cause to remember that special day
I think what a sudden, sudden ordering that fire made of the Southtown,
Celebrating my seventh birthday.

WALKER EVANS'S "ALABAMA COTTON TENANT FARMER'S WIFE, 1936"

for Mark and Marriann Callahan

She has made what she could out of this life.
It is spare
But she bites her lips,
Perhaps, tastes her own blood
And knows she will endure.
It looks as if the wind has worn away her beauty
As it has torn away the paint from their clap-board dwelling.
It is the desolate thirties.
The land has long since turned from yielding cotton.
She has Modigliani eyes
They cut through,
They look forward
The time is spent for this brief picture taking.
She will make what she can for dinner
And hold on to what love she has in Alabama.

WALKER EVANS'S "ALABAMA TENANT FARMER, 1936"

There was once hope in my eyes,
As fresh as my newborn's cries.
She is my survivor; she will break free
From the thinness of dimes,
From the dirt which has insinuated its way
Past skin, blood, and bone to some deeper place
Where even the soul has not thought to go.
My daughter is my last gamble;
She will free me from these hills.
She is my way out. I have turned the land
For the very last time. I can do no more,
Nor hope that this marketable year will turn more
Plentiful profit. In the late night when the house
Breathes in silence, I taste my wife's subtle
Passion; while she can still taste the sun
In my pores. A stone is in me which is blind
To that which I once called hope.

A CHILDHOOD MEMORY

I found a world in the small stones
In the black alleys of Birmingham, Alabama,
Among the papers, bottles, and cans which
Were thrown or blown under the houses
Where we used to play hide and seek
With the neighborhood girls who, when
They were caught with their fingers
Uncrossed, or who maybe uncrossed them
Intentionally, had to lift their dresses
As punishment until we saw their best secret.
Our inexperienced eyes glazed in wonder.
In the space of that one moment our fingers
Relaxed and the girls trapped us
And down came our pants
And up went our embarrassed vanity.
Sometimes the older boys said
They had capitalized on such advantages,
And that we younger boys had yet to learn
Of the explosive sweetness of our desires.
What wonder there was in those games,
Discovering what lay beneath our basic skins.

SATURDAY AFTERNOON

I manicure the lawn because the neighbors have all done theirs
And ours is still too long from the last Fall that my wife bows
Her head every time we leave the house and says:
"I will not lift my head until our lawn looks perfect,
Then I will be able to smile at our neighbors who have nothing
To do but cut their lawns twice a week and sun themselves in between."
I know I will not finish the lawn today. Projects get put aside;
There is never enough time. Now, I must cancel this cutting
Because a thunderstorm is coming. This is the third week.
The thunder is being challenged by Air Force maneuvers.
The old man across the street is conducting his own maneuvers.
His wife has questioned some unacceptable rule.
He raises his hand as lightning flashes. Thunder follows.
More thunder follows the husband's present.
It is a gift she has never welcomed. She blames heaven.
It has never interceded nor once saw fit to hear her private pleas.
This Saturday she knows the defense is in her hands.
She makes her way to her Spring kitchen where her hands
Take firm grasp of the tea pot. She flings it in rebuttal;
Retreat comes too late. Heaven fingers lightning over the house.
An ambulance screams after the pain has arrived.
Now the old woman excels in silence.
She will accomplish her tasks
As she has always done, and hope someday when she lifts her face
She will have the privilege of seeing my wife's eyes proudly.

PENNY POSTCARD

I am searching through the antique dust of this old shop.
My fingers stumble across a postcard written when I was
Ten years old and still a native of Birmingham, Alabama.
Mrs. Frisch is determined to pass on the latest family
News. This is what she had to say:

Dear Florine:

I heard from Alvin; he didn't write much; he did receive my pkg; he
had his hair cut short   about a half inch and was feeling fine, or so he
says and would drop us a line when he   arrives in L. He said he was
hog-tied and ham-strung from being kept in that camp for   two
and a half months. So there will be no gifts coming. He, also, said not
to worry or to   write or send anything until he writes us. I,
personally, don't think he can receive pkgs   where he is. Junior
Bill came home last Wed. He looks mighty grand. I bet all the girls in
the neighborhood think so too. He was home on a one day pass. No
telling how much   damage he's done, he has fifty-five days to go,
and then he will get his cadet uniform. I   only hope he makes
it. God only knows. Finally. If you don't come home next Sat. I will
send you Alvin's letter, although I have told you everything he said.

Love, Mother

All of this traveled a long distance on a penny postcard two years
before we brought the Germans and the Japanese to their proverbial
knees. War like that one is unforgivable.

EARLY WARNINGS
for Betty Jennings
Friend, Teacher

Rosemary Featherstone (no one will believe that was her name a hundred years from now) always began our first day in Homeroom at the beginning of the year by saying, "You must put your shoulders to the wheel and push three quarters of the way with vigor and persistence and then you can coast the fourth quarter to the end. It is foolhardy to try it any other way." This was the way she ended her advice. "You will be out of energy if you try to do it any other way. Use your energy wisely the first time." We never did. I am not sure that any of her students ever did. We were young and foolhardy; we knew better.

I know I thought I knew better when the old women of our house used to warn me about getting too close to the fire when the old men were beginning to bar-b-que. "Smoke follows the ugly," they would imply. Since I was younger and smarter I thought I didn't have to pay attention, but then I would end up crying vigorously when my eyes filled with blinding smoke. Disobedience was my reward; I would learn this years later remembering I had been warned against attracting the smoke just as generous Mrs. Featherstone had sought to warn us against inaction and how to seize those special moments.

MEMORY IS THE BRAILLE THE WIND LEAVES
for Richard and Naomi Baron

It is a startling year now, since your early morning call.
Was the bell in my dream? Was it a wrong lover's call?
Who, who was it in the timeless morning, calling?
I cannot remember the scene or warmth.
I know it is impossible to reconstruct a dream.
It is the image which takes us by surprise.
It was the fabric of surrender in your voice.
It was a voice that still carried but one color.
The years taught me how dog-eared that voice had become.
Even the comfort it once offered was wearing thin.
What was the urgent resolve that you had to tell me?
Had you been forced to such a decision by expensive pain?
What could I offer you but the promise
Of making the transition of home to *home?*
Is this how you wanted to round out your 365 days?
A vow is a promise hard as stone,
Soft as mist, sharp as splintered crystal.
It is a cold February that I wrap and brace you against.
Yours is an unfathomable pain I cannot see.
It eats of the flesh from the inside.
Eyes with a deeper sense of vision must look
Beyond your ability to feel.
Your dark eyes work to read the braille the wind leaves.
We located a physician from the Far East;
He did not have any safeguards against pain.
We were left our own human reserve.
We went back to where we began: *home*
And tried to think how we could begin again.

CSONTVARY TIVADAR'S "OLD WOMAN PEELING AN APPLE"
for Toth Edit

I have heard it said that the apple is woman's failure.
I do not know which man first wrongly deposited that
Statement in the infectious air. Perhaps it came
From the tongues of poisonous snakes because they
Were enthralled by the dark curiosity in women's eyes,
It is a light like no other. I, on the other hand,
Have peeled apples like a careful profession
Since I was seven years old. I have fed
Some astounding hungers with them; I have pared
Their skins thinly and boiled them for jellies,
Sliced the meat from the core to make turnovers,
Pies, and sweet sauces. I have dried the new seeds,
Planted them but not with much success.
Nothing new has ever come from them. Now my skin
Darkens like peeled apples. I am eighty years into
This process; I use my skills to stay alive.
My husband was never as cautious as I learned to be.
He never paused to consider what portions I afforded
Him, or what he carelessly left on his plate.
He ate on the run; he died on the run.
That day the house was filled with the aroma of herbs
On the other hand, I have never followed his mark.
I never make haste; I am deliberate.
I shall die with this attitude.
So you my grandson must never acknowledge
What I tell you with shame. It is the inheritance
I leave you. You will want, I hope, to be a different man;
To move through your home tasting, seeing, and breathing
The passionate textures of those around you, as well as
The flavors of all the things you have gathered.

INSTRUCTIONS

My mother used to cook magnificently with her two endowed hands. Then the suddenness of an illness stroked her body, leaving her left side dead and her right side maintaining a vivid life style. She went on cooking with her good right hand. She often declared: "Don't let nothing inanimate ever, ever defeat you." Although she had twenty-twenty sight, in the end, she would succumb to invisible cancer because she did not see it coming like a freight train, which she could have let pass her by without so much as a kind "Good day to you," if it hadn't insisted on making her personal acquaintance and taking up fatal residence in her bones. My mother was never one for casual chitchat. She would give each individual, if he or she merited it, a proper Christian greeting and then move on to the daily gray surrounding her life.

SEX EDUCATION

It is true that no one in the black Baptist Church ever sung or talked about sex, not in any manner a straightforward way or surreptitiously a quiet way for that matter. It was something unique that we would have to discover on our own, like the answers to a particularly expensive math test which costs so much in pain that you are never able to feel any relief in your brain afterwards or quietly say "ouch" reflecting the degree of pain or "ouch" so quietly that it could not disturb nor rattle the holy peace. No one ever asks "why?" All of our discoveries are left to be found in the local, black river called Freedom, which runs naked through the middle of town, funny as that may seem. It must have been thought that sex was a blight or the mystery we search all our married life to invent. Some deacon must have thought that the young would discover it as one discovers gold, or the goal one hopes to achieve, and that the answers would be found by some miraculous fumble or stumble through the dark of fascinating intimacy, an expression of dedicated creativity leading to untold happiness like some announced newlyweds who have been strictly told by the pastor that "marriage is an estate not to be entered into lightly." Such a pronouncement coming at the end of a wedding ceremony always sent me into a philosophical slump. Now this is as much of an exposé as I wish to indulge in because the matter, as far as I can see, is fundamentally clear and full of song, both secular and spiritual music of the two beat kind, "Baby" and "Lordy." You simply have to remember where you are and whether it's Saturday night or Sunday morning: dance hall or church service. Scott would ask himself why years later, tired to death when everything emotional had been rung, dry as love, from the experience. No one ever told him love would be as difficult as learning to play the piano, which, in all likelihood, can be interesting if the player has any angry energy on his fingers despite the fact that he may be tired of the wonderful carrot color which had always dominated his once loneliness all filled with sadness peaceable as the world is without Elvis or those who follow the tree of his career as if he were still available to ride a horse as if, knight like he could secure the peace for a time, like drinking beer and sparkling beauty at the same time. He learned late in life that your mother had said he would never marry you. That announcement was the blight of his future. You will not choose what is always destined. You will undertake mysteries you never dreamed could possibly exist. You were the food he would never eat with any sense of peacefulness; he dreamed in dressing you in peaceful fame, the light of diamonds; he wanted to dress you in the lauds of envy. He would have dressed you in his achievement but who of us are willing to wait a lifetime for such a thing to happen? Sex, however poetic, was not uppermost in his mind, he sought the marlin of his life; he would have struggled like the old man taking vengeance to prove that he is a worthy man. He would hang his marlin high in the blazing air like a question mark, boring as it may seem like hate which makes the air vibrate, so that you will see the waves being spun from the exhaust of a Space Shuttle.

NIGHTHAWKS

A clinical beauty radiates through the windows of this diner.
It has invited a few passing guests for the night.
The lone attendant serves cups of loneliness.
The conversation is spare.
A late-night lady is courted by the vanity of her belief.
A man with his last cigarette waits for the waiter to offer coffee.
He tastes the loneliness of sleep.
He will not know himself in the morning.
He will see an image of himself as true and flimsy in the mirror.
He will brush away the night's slight encounter.
He will head off to the cemetery of work
where the clarity of last night will haunt how they
casually disappeared, never giving thought
to what the morning would tell them.
Light falls on their bodies like casual ermine.
Her name is Rose; his name is Austere.
The mystery is in her name, honor cloaks his.
Something approaching love can be blamed
on the coffee they drank that night,
and the spare words they uttered in that place.
They retain the flavor of what they both tasted.
Now he is awake from the wrestle of body and sheets.
She is quiet beneath the cover of light.
Their bare legs are soothed by the morning air.
They will remember the rub of ecstasy,
the tease of love on their skin.
Such nightmares exist in the places where sleep
abandons momentary acquaintances.

AMERICAN GOTHIC

There is no southern record of my mother or father standing next to each other with uncommon grace like these two stand. If they were next to each other it was with the pitch forks aimed solidly at each other's heart. If fate contrived to have them stand next to each other it was out of the predestined fear that they could do nothing to alter their position or condition. They were there, as we are all here, inextricably bound by our different natures to the spaces we must occupy. There is no northern record that they slept comfortably next to each other. There were never any muffled sounds in my nightmares. What were their lives like: work, eating for renewed strength, sleep, and then work again? So what would they think of me now making poems out of their indifference without the slightest recognition for space, time, community, love, or personal house to thresh out their spare lives in?

THE FACE'S SPECTRUM

My wife confronts me with what she asserts is the truth of my self-
absorption, my unfamiliarity with the spectrum of my emotions.
Suddenly, I know not many individuals are equipped to read the faces
of the men and women they meet daily. In this way, I am fortunate
enough to confound my enemies. It is a reliable truth that my
mother taught me by inference never to reveal to my left hand what
the right had accomplished. That way blinders were always placed on
my eyes as well.

I remember, interestingly enough, a friend informing me that I was
in love with his lover, when in fact the exact opposite was true,
I was in love with him. I am constantly amazed how effectively I
have hidden my subterranean motives; they are, after all, my private
treasures. Either I am richly growing in interest or I am truly
bankrupt in knowing my mind. What I do know is there is no denying
the truths which exist in other people's minds. What I do know from
these two instances is that they do not know of the widespread
tentacles of my feelings.

I take my surprises as they come: apples and kumquats.
I am amazed that there are too few oranges and persimmons.
And when happiness envelopes me in cantaloupe skin
I do not allow my body to respond with the amazement of taste
for fear that the joy will dissipate sooner than expected and turn
sour. So I am amazed when my wife tells me that a friend advised
her long ago that I was not faring well and that I needed her
feminine embrace. I think how little that friend knew of the powers
of my endurance. I have in me the blood of slaves.

cousin lou took care of us. still we worried her to death with questions and drunkenness. her weeks were methodically organized. i am amazed that we stumbled along without her careful, religious guiding hand. she was the stabilizer. she washed clothes on mondays long after she had sent the men off to work. billy and I were ushered off to school. she ironed on tuesday. she daily cleaned the house and cooked every healthy day of her life until she was so ill she could not lift her hands and was forced to breathe stones. wednesday was always her catch-up day. there was nothing, in the interim, to do in the back alley of avenue h. but wait for her justified end to finally come. when she had taken her last breath and we had rendered our severe tears we removed every article from the front room. death forced us to do the cleaning before the church members came with black crape and hung it over the entrance of our house. crape spoke of the death which had oc-curred. the sisters and brothers of christ did the same elaborately at the church and when we took her body from the front room where everyone had come and paid their honor. they rang the bells to our solemn march as the hefty coffin rose on the shoulders of the good deacons and we fol-lowed close behind holding each other's grief. in those foreign days flowers came from the black corners of the city. their fragrance was a sedative for our unaccountable loss. they were the handkerchief for our weeping and the blanket for our cries. the church ushers were always present with fans to quell and cool our shouting when the preacher told those of us who had survived how much we would miss the small things she had done for us. death would make us realize the irreplaceable absence he had willingly granted us. in those days we put the flowers in the ground with the casket. they were too costly for someone to come and take from the grave. only family and friend were allowed to take memorial cuttings to be placed in the bible to remember the dead. we left the cemetery with only a prayer to dismiss the faithful. jazz was for sinners, the wayward, and the lost, so for the time being we would leave this holy ground to take solace in the scripture of chapter and verse. After several months had elapsed we would return, recite those learned passages, place a marble stone on your head, and let it, finally, say your name.

THE MOTHER OF THE NEIGHBORHOOD

Son, I tell you there comes a time for atonement, even when you are feeling most dreary trying to work at your computer with a certain mild contentment that is always fulfilling when you think you have done your best work and will earn or win, which is even better, a trip long dreamed of to Hawaii because you made an unexpected and fantastic bogey on the eighteenth hole like any professional would accomplish in a crunch because he could see the thunder coming and feel the local river rising toward flood stage beyond what one might ordinarily call an aberration because the monsoon like rage is only experienced in India which is also my name because under the influence of pain my mother thought that India sounded like a pretty name. Mothers are given to pretty.

What could I do having arrived like a slow burning rocket upon re-entry looking for the softest chair to land in and call home because as a new-born infant I do not have all of the mobility that I would acquire in later years nor all of the sincerity my mother would teach me to employ as if I were serving scrumptious desserts for the comfortable and uncomfortable relatives who because of past experiences were unsure of the nature of my invitation or whether they should be here at all? But that is the way it is with experiences and especially with relatives so I always have nautical books with which each one can invest their imaginations in.

This submarine blessed with ancient purple has become our Russian pyramid, the place where we are sealed in forever with what goods we could manage to salvage and take with us on this final foreign journey. We surely did not envision this sinking as our final act. Tonight I arrive at home at the end of the day and know that I am finishing the first Spring day at the beginning of the Twenty-First Century and to mark this occasion is an announcement that a twenty-year-old man has experimented with the sumptuous joy that can be obtained from the new velocity of amphetamines which are growing like raspberries in great clusters across the country like the chautauquas sprung up across the land when the citizens desired voluminous knowledge of different onomatopoetic gardens like those which our first Eve pruned, picked, and gently admired. It is that first kindness which makes us hopeful that love like a wildflower fantasy will spring in the minds of local lumberjacks and blacksmiths who ascend into orbit under ordinary moonlight having freed themselves from the bondage of mere survival transforming themselves and their tools into joy, grace, dreams, and music. The rave of the tiger is a grief beyond any death this youth could have imagined and beyond the empty renewal this Spring brings without his footprints wonderful in his mother's garden or the perspicacious holiday voice he could have uttered with unimaginable hope or imagination. His death leaves his soulmate who possessed no oracular sight as the ancient Greeks did or even the Biblical prophets maintained to keep a people just and a community solid. I leap with a giraffe's love into a violet morality. The first ark horse had a similar freedom. My blood thins like air; I walk calmly in thirty-second steps toward deserved retirement. The bottom of the watermelon is green tranquility beautiful as the first apple or the red desirous fox. There is a car parked on grass turning orange as a carrot. It is a corvette. Please, no thanks. What we see before us is a kind of balloon that is filled with sunny happiness. You may say that this is all balderdash but I perceive in it a joy quiet as a voluptuous tomato who without the slightest blink of its holiday red, can ridicule or complain mississauga, a sunny creative cast.

THE ANCHOR OF RAINBOWS

The motive of my anger is not grace abounding unreliable and dependent which falls inexorably from somewhere not unlike space wherein you cannot breathe easily nor taste in the air a presence which is sandalwood scenting the marble of holy places that age with a grace no flesh can emulate or hope to be. Flesh is all batter and flaccid mixture, wordless incantations emblazoned on the air before all banquets festive and otherwise. This is the formula for my rages. Take your several promises and grind them into miller's flour fine as sunlight dust. Add three lies turned red, then black from air, from too much exposure, too much light all at once in a dark and cool place. Add a flock of personages all bringing with them the violence of their inheritance, shaking themselves as if they were free of ancestral curses. My mother always said "Never let a woman in your house first thing on Monday mornings." She comes to shed all of her tribulations from the conch of her muscular goodwill all symmetrical and filled with striations that geese leave when they are escaping wherever they have just been and do not know what colors tomorrow holds. The sky is terror for them and still they must soar through it; the wind is fear and still it must support their every endeavor; their wings are brushes making known the opaline clouds and the blue beneath; their feet must discover the earth browns while their beaks must crack the film like glazes of wind. I am a goose among cabbages, flagrant as the morning sun creeping like a predator hidden beneath the flimsy opaline of clouds. Sun is molten Phoenix always in the process of saying goodbye world filled with wonderful angers, immaculate hates, and infinite causes to rejoice about some inevitable failure of peaches, the brilliant skins of marmalades, the crevices of ferment turning into pillow frivolous wines which old women craft from eggs and stars and butterflies, carefully shaded under black umbrellas which keeps the laser rays of sun from searing the wines of passion and dreams. These old women born of cold absence and innocent and dead galaxies that have become all darkness withering into a supple spindle, a shift of moon that will give the night nothing but radiant mares who cavort beneath the skin of their farms in dazzling sequences that are always perennial. Horses are stars dancing on the horizon of the eyes; they make their yearly pilgrimages to the sacred places of the earth. The flask they bring is enormous and pristine as they plunge the symmetry of the container beneath the shoulders of jeweled waters. I am in these streets learning the sweet clientele like the lazy grasshopper who gathers only summer cherries and casts scorn upon the winter potatoes like the bird whose feathers are born of specific prejudices which I am forced to learn to inhabit like the space of rock as it anchors rainbows.

DREAMING OF THE SOUTH IN A SINGLE BREATH

We gave ourselves over to cornbread and love
but never to fate who turned herself into the
watery attention of sharks, leap of dolphins
or the land-bound rabbits or the caged sad
chickens who will never be as free as the
undocumented mermaid who has the song of a
jaguar caught in her throat that is as long
and melodic as a giraffe's neck and stamped
with a final seal which holds like the
mysterious glue of a stradavarius violin
or tuned as tight as a cat's gut or the
lovely smell of a hibiscus whose bloom
happens late after the mid-day sun and
whose perfumes wafts into the dining
room window, adding sudden flavors to
the evening meal. This is what love
might have been for us if I had been
willing to take a concrete chance on
the future, but I failed, and so all
of my dog-day-miracle fortunes were
changed in that dazzling moment when
both family and friend realized that
I had not a single inkling about what
love meant, nor what the possibility
of what it might do in the infinite future
or what hope might bring in the month of a hot
shiftless June which seemed to fall off
my shoulders like a silk negligee
which always cries out "look!" "see!"
what your imaginary body might have
been if you had gambled on the
breakable chances which were offered
in a small, rather ostentatious way like
precious china or razor-thin porcelain
in the voice of a pretender king who
has only to sail out on his own financed

ship to the new world across the golden
waves of Neptune's world as quiet as
a cat in a midnight library reading
a seriously funny novel which grows
toward an unexpected conclusion
like a flower which takes a hundred
years to bloom like that sudden
blooming which occurs the lungs
screeching "YO!" but that's like
the single heroic woman who thinks
she can swim the entire whangdoodle
ocean slivering thin as white clouds
which invade the mind like the slim
excruciatingly bright solar light
which touches the tongue with a
scrumptdilectious smell like the
hair from my son's head long
before he begins to consider
worrying about the loss of his
full head of golden means soft
and wispy as cotton candy but
not as sticky or as captivating
as any thing with a brightly
colored panda flaming like a
supercalifragilisticexpiali-
docious quilt whose weight
sounds like the incessant
cricket whose chatter is a
game to destroy whatever
sanity the mind might achieve
like love or justice or
the foolish reparations
much of the world thinks it
can buy off for the terrible
sweet sins it has committed
and continues to commit against
jesus flowers serendipity and the
laughter which comes through the nose
great forever with inspiration and

curiosity like the numbers the old
black used to top place just before
vacation hoping to hit enough to
stave off hunger for a month or two
the strict way the mystery of love
which only the cool possess because
they understand where the folds
of peace emanate from.

THE PIANO TEACHER'S LIVING ROOM
for Phyllis Katz

Father after father came there
year after exhausting year,
without the slightest pretensions
because her house, for an hour,
was filled with a strict calm;
the couch invited patient sleep
with no emotional demands required.
She could do it all:
teach their children nuanced rhythms,
accomplish miracles of steady sound,
sweet melodies which evoked
harmonic chills on the skin.
All of this voiced from the
smallest fingertips while
fathers nodded in the living room.
She asked her students' hands to speak
controlled pianissimos, which they
had never imagined was within
the reach of their ordinary days.
I marvel at how, week after tedious hour
she got them to caress the sanctity of air,
and make it shimmer without ever disturbing
the well-needed sleep of their fathers.

174

SHARECROPPER

His hands were rough potatoes;
The fields knew them well.
His skin was fierce. *sunburnt*
The sun blazed high on his work
Raining down noonday sweat.
At evening he moved
Toward the clarity of water and
Its naturally clear potential
To remove the lumps of earth *dirt on his*
Grown on his hands that day. *hands and clothes*
In his fresh clothes
Filled with the food his wife made,
The fresh words they spoke to each other
On the porch in the evening seemed
A solemn accomplishment
Under the rejoicing stars.

SLEEPING LOVERS

There they were positioned in the waiting room of the local
bus station, asleep in each other's arms, when suddenly,
without warning, they were instant gasoline and flames.
Fire itched into their flesh like the tight curls on his dark neck,
and the long, straight ones which dangled like gold from her fair head.
It was the abidingly cool smell of the gasoline
and the joyful fire's tickle that caused these two
to dance wildly like Holiness Witnesses
fingered by the Holy Ghost, like puppets in a conflagration
until they fell, smothering each other on the ground in
a heap of flesh, hair, blood, and bare bones, becoming
collector's items, someone's common vision, a naked
brutality, the general hostility of a father's father's
father's teachings. These lovers did not exit this life
singing into a peaceful cinematic sunset. They had one
utterable and civilized love. It was tested with flames
by these certain youths who made, in that terminal, a dark
monument to Siegfried and Brunhilde while listening to the
song of secrecy propagated by a father's father's father's
father's laughter.

HUSBAND WANTED

None but those with the following refined qualities need apply: *you must possess the ability to tickle silk; you need not possess the static cling of electricity; you must be willing to love any woman named julie ann pizza and enter her life with hat in hand preferably riding a palomino of distinguished breed vowing to be a party to everything the horse is inclined to do; you must hate zits and do everything possible to eradicate them from the body politic; you must love bubble gum and children on hot blue days as well as those days which are exactly opposite because I am a woman who requires it. I do not wish to present myself as niggling on the subject; I want to be clear and non-deceptive, otherwise there would be no wisdom whatsoever in my having paid for this advertisement.*

GREASY SUNSHINE

I know you to be
the voluptuous
woman you claim
to be. I would like
to torpedo your
underbelly with
the last car found
in Texas. The only
cow I own will
come and tweak
the gloomy
sunshine white
as mayonnaise
on a slice of
stingy republican
bread, that costs
less than a walnut
or its wrinkled
façade dried like
a psychedelic light.
It is true that
I try to ferret out
the envy in nature
which will happily
mirror the beach
or a sweet traitor,
who has covered
the promise of
his heart with
a chartreuse
handkerchief.

RWANDA # 1

This woman's body is blistered with death.
Soon her swollen arms will break her bonds;
The heated water of her body will splay
The ground where she lies and bless it.
Her head lies five feet away from her body
Screaming silence. The dust of revolution
Chokes her mouth. Her eyes bleed sunlight.
Sweet death is the harvest of this land.
This woman is but one victim who ran
As far as she could to escape the machete
Which with one immaculate swing severed
Her body from its intangible soul.
Who in this village, seeing such a sight,
Dare speak, with a civilized tongue
Forbidding the earth to welcome another
Living being into corruption?

RWANDA # 2

I have eaten the geography of meridians and longitudes
There is no north which will lead me to safety
To the place which gave birth to me.
The crust of snow has been sifted with blood
A white temperature locks my teeth.
My throat is the fastest luge ever!
Speed melts the sizzling ice.
Winners are duly cheered
There is no generous way to arrive at success.

RWANDA # 3

I have eaten the last of the evening's snow
A white temperature locks my teeth
My throat is a fast luge tunnel
The ribbon that marks the winner
Is lost in the celebration of my stomach.
There is no match for the darkness there;
Snowlight is a flood on space;
Speed melts the sizzling ice.

RWANDA # 4

Four black men swing in the dancing air
They are connected by an electrical thread
An acrid smell tells me they are dead
Their spirits sing of a time
That was greenly sad and unfair
Theirs is a song willed to the wind
Who can document their offense,
Their human sin? Who among us
Can sing of joy with our feet bound,
Our hands tied behind our backs?

RWANDA # 5

The trees looked starved;
Their leaves are gone.
The youngest of the flowers
Lie strewn and dead in the roads.
The neighbors, who are left,
Take staggering breaths and
Continue to breathe beneath
The dark burden of their eyelids.
There are no bright solutions.
Only the dark may be severed by lightning.
Its energy surpasses the true explanations,
How these times and angers knotted themselves
In the back and in the neck
Growing into incurable tumors.
The bread I bake is made of blood and earth;
Its taste is withered leaf and dry bark.

RWANDA # 6

John Deere shovels bite into the ground
They unearth huge trenches
They lift large stacks of bodies
And plant them side by side.
The land is covered over,
Seeded with new grass and trees.
No one can repair the air.
This is a place of rest.
No one can repair the air.
The rain baptizes; silt weds rock.
A new balm is prescribed
For all the pains left behind.

RWANDA # 7
Instant Replay

With easy malice one African severs another man's head.
The ground sprouts bodies like rotting potatoes.
There is no water here; the land is dry and begging.
The eyes are astonished continents away.
The heart trembles then stops; the machete has no blood
of its own. Where is the rain and snow that cleanses?

A body writhes in the dust; its head toils in the river.
The river laughs; the land has nothing to say.
I shall remember these deaths with praises and psalms;
I feel their spirits winding themselves around the roots
of trees. There will be no bountiful harvests this year.
I gather the instant replays of stalks and twigs and
empty things.

And he, who I thought was my neighbor, came with swift and easy hate in his hands, cleft my head from my soul, as I knelt in the dust of our homeland. What spite the land has come to that it should so rage against human nature! Have we not kicked enough stones together? Why has love turned the air to such an expense? Where are the waters of cooling passions? My bloated self is rooted in contagion. Ancient angers spread in small rashes. Nothing can ease the interminable itch which attacks the land. Poison seeps from an open boil. If you try to lance it, it disappears from one section of the body and reappears in another. Poison becomes the texture of the wind. I was once rock, bark, earthen jar, and moonlight. Now I am fresh sun and rotting flesh. These antique angers which belonged to my neighbor and to his father are mine now by death and default. Pain is the machete that bit into my life so swift and clean it never tasted blood or stained itself. My body pours itself into the mouth of the earth. It feels the thunder of hurrying feet wandering into a foreign darkness. The wealth of the nation is silent; it offers no rescue. The pieties of food and shelter are useless. The sun has left the land, the water is foul with intestines. What strange white peace is it which approaches on the wind rising as it must from the sea?

RWANDA # 9

This salve of youthful blood
Balms the sores of the country.
Still she does not heal;
The wound is too great.
The pulse runs in halting breaths
Too hard to draw.
The trees weep their leaves;
Water washes over dry tubers.
The tender wood is exposed
To lice and vermin;
Gray worms exit the body.
The river gives an embrace
To the floating bodies.
Who among the dead
Can bury the dead?
The land has lost
Its sweet negotiations.
We turn the earth;
Nothing is there.
Slowly the land
Recedes into water.
There are no sacred prayers
Found in its folds.
The sun, the last
Of our martyrs
Is dead.

RWANDA # 10

The cranes have come;
A steam shovel bites
Into the natural ground.
Old earth is pushed aside,
It lies in large mounds
As if some gigantic ant
Had burrowed up toward light.
Random bushes, grass, and a single
Stalk of corn begins to grow here.
The men plant steel rods, girders,
Cinder blocks, then cement floors.
They are making rooms
In the spacious air
For new tenants.
The girders are covered,
Wired, and walled in
With hammered sound.
Inside there is a schedule,
Outside a deadline to meet.
The rain washes the earth,
The silt flows away.
Someone will make passage here,
Take flights like breaths
Of human motion.

DEFECTIVE VILLANELLE

There was a time when the black men ate first
because the field's work demanded a full stomach.
Then we children held our laughter and smiles

under the strict moratorium of our mother's eyes
lest we unwittingly disturbed our father's sleep.
That was the time when the black men ate first,

while our secondary stomachs whined and complained
(the justice of the scraps left for us to consume),
like children forced to hold their laughter and smiles

because the times required it. We needed to be quiet.
Whatever was necessary, the black men brought it home,
and that was the time when the working men ate first.

As persuasive as ever, our joyous voices made noises
outside the house, in the yards and streets, carefully
as children pressured to hold their laughter and smiles.

Our bright voices could raise the roof of a black sky
(and not betray any of us who had never understood
this was the 30s and 40s when black men ate first),
like children who unleashed their laughter and smiles.

FIVE VARIATIONS OF SILENCE

I .
A butcher's hatchet falls;
a white annoys the ground
the fall has a pungent scent.
Sleep is an engraved
invitation to death.

II
The dead have antiseptic faces,
Sterilized bodies, quiet command.
Death is the presence
of final sleep, a consort
that collects all dares,
debits, and interests.

III
Silence moves in veiled degrees;
touch is the temperature of
its invisible motion.
Smell is the sum of all its gestures;
the tongue soaks them up like cool water.

IV
Silence is a canopy of anguish,
a deeper earthly shade
that suffers no third party.

V
The grave is an open ache,
a dry pain. Light falls there
like a thundered breath.

DRIVE-BY DEATHS

There are bullets flying,
The daily neighborhood
Shrapnel on a battlefield.
Not safe to walk down the street,
Nothing but music on your mind;
Beware, there may be a bomb planted,
Waiting for a right foot to trigger it.
Believe me we must get from home to work
And back again and most days we make it.

ATLANTA

sifts its burnished earth
looking for one diamond fact
that can cut through to the hard truth,
one connecting link of hair,
one human tissue,
a drop of blood, a traceable footstep,
a single pin that can sharply point
toward the deeply guilty, one thread which
can attach these youthful deaths together.

BLACK JAZZ

Grandfather's eyes burned black jazz
Like coals brightening the fireplace.
He played trumpet
With the smallest community of air
Ever imprisoned in human lungs.
When he played
The walls clapped for joy.
The breath he blew
Made the house sway,
And our hearts tremble
Like the unstable floors
We walked upon.

WOMAN WITH DARK EYES

Wonder is written in her eyes
Three children are her frame
Her face is encouragement
The plains are ingrained in her skin
The southern territories in her face
Her lips whisper to the palms
My fingers memorize her voice
I keep her secrets
Will not let water touch them
Nor fresh earth bury them
Lady with the dark eyes
Your children memorize you